Journey to Inner Space

Journey to Inner Space

Rodney R. Romney

Abingdon
Nashville

Journey to Inner Space

Copyright © 1980 by Abingdon

All rights reserved.
No part of this book may be reproduced in any manner whatsoever without written permission of the publisher except brief quotations embodied in critical articles or reviews. For information address Abingdon, Nashville, Tennessee.

Library of Congress Cataloging in Publication Data
ROMNEY, RODNEY R 1931-
  Journey to inner space.
    1. Meditation. 2. Spiritual life. I. Title.
BV4813.R59   248'.3   79-18822
                ISBN 0-687-20590-5

Scripture quotations in this publication are from the Revised Standard Version of the Bible, copyrighted 1946, 1952, © 1971, 1973 by the Division of Christian Education of the National Council of the Churches of Christ in the U.S.A., and used by permission. Many verses have been paraphrased. Quotation from *Markings,* by Dag Hammarskjold, translated by Leif Sjoberg and W. H. Auden. Copyright © 1964 by Alfred A. Knopf, Inc.

MANUFACTURED BY THE PARTHENON PRESS AT
NASHVILLE, TENNESSEE, UNITED STATES OF AMERICA

*Dedicated to the people of the
Lakeshore Avenue Baptist Church
in Oakland, California, who have
given me both freedom and companionship
on the spiritual path to the inner kingdom.*

Contents

Chapter 1 A Lonely Journey..................................9
Chapter 2 Exploration into God.........................19
Chapter 3 The Way-Shower...............................27
Chapter 4 An Instinct for the Infinite.................37
Chapter 5 Ceiling Prayers..................................46
Chapter 6 Freedom Through Surrender...........55
Chapter 7 The Greater Love..............................62
Chapter 8 Let There Be Light............................72
Chapter 9 The Meditation Experience..............81
Chapter 10 The Ladder of Prayer.......................95
Chapter 11 A Night in the Hills........................109
           (a Meditation on the Lord's Prayer
           and Psalm 23)
Chapter 12 Water from Deep Wells.................121
           Benedictus, a Final Good Word.............140

The longest journey
Is the journey inwards.
Of him who has chosen his destiny,
Who has started upon his quest
For the source of his being.

—**Dag Hammarskjold**

Chapter 1
A Lonely Journey

As I begin writing this, my mind runs back across the span of twenty-four springs to a time when I was cast in a college production of Christopher Fry's play *A Sleep of Prisoners* (Oxford University Press, 1951). In this play four soldiers are held prisoners in a church, where, through dreams, each speaks what at heart he is. In the final part the dreams change to a state of thought shared by all the men, which is also the theme of the play, articulated by Private Tim Meadows:

> The human heart can go to the lengths of God.
> Dark and cold we may be, but this
> Is no winter now. The frozen misery
> Of centuries breaks, cracks, begins to move,
> The thunder is the thunder of the floes,
> The thaw, the flood, the upstart Spring.
> Thank God our time is now when wrong
> Comes up to face us everywhere,
> Never to leave us till we take
> The longest stride of soul men ever took.
> Affairs are now soul size.
> The enterprise
>   Is exploration into God, . . .
> Where are you going? It takes
> So many thousand years to wake,
> But will you wake for pity's sake?

Those words stand as a challenge to me today, a challenge to go beyond all histrionic limitations and to face the alembic of my soul, its own exploration into God.

I awoke one morning not long ago from that quiescent state of half sleep and half wakefulness with a dream surfaced in my consciousness. Before it could begin to evanesce, as dreams often do, I struggled to focus on it with greater acuity than I normally give to dreams, for I had the feeling I was in touch with something soul size, and I wanted to hold and study it.

In my dream I was struggling up the side of a steep mountain. Although there seemed to be many others standing at intervals on my pathway, I was the only one trying to go anywhere. The mists hung low, casting a moist gray shadow over the trees and shrubs that loomed beside my path like grotesque chimeras, bedizened with a slimy, silvery moss. Occasionally this moss entangled itself in my hair and clothing and delayed my progress. The faces of those persons who occasionally lined the edge of my path to observe my progress were grave, obdurate, unmoved to any expressions of pity or sympathy. I felt alone with the utter aloneness one feels in some miasma of a wasteland, and I felt uncomfortable and awkward under those piercing eyes. Yet I could not halt my precipitate climb up that mountain slope.

Suddenly to the side of my path there appeared a protective shelter. At first I discerned it to be a crude log hut, similar to the one my father had built in the mountains of northeastern Idaho where he had lived most of his years as a miner. Then the cabin changed into a sleek shelter of steel and plastic, such as one sees at bus stops where passengers may stand protected from inclement weather while waiting for a bus. And quickly that faded into a religious shrine, similar to those I had often viewed along the roadsides in rural France when I lived there for a year.

At that point I ceased to give attention to the shelter at

all, for I now became aware that within it were many recognizable faces—my wife, my mother, other members of my family, friends and people from my church, even some dear ones who had died. Some persons I did not know or recognize were also there, and their expressions were warm and sympathetic. They were holding out their hands to me, as though inviting me to come inside and rest. I paused for a few moments beside that wayside shelter, and they surged toward me as one body. For a few brief, exulting moments I seemed to be lifted in their arms and passed gently around that circle. I had the sensation of being rocked from outstretched arm to outstretched arm. Above all, I felt the elation of being enfolded in a milieu of incredible love, sheltered and protected from the stern, grave countenances that had earlier watched my torturous ascent up that mountain trail.

Then everything faded except the path. I stood again in its center, this time absolutely alone. The atmosphere had changed. The mists were now beneath me. I could look back and see that the way I had previously come was still enshrouded in heavy clouds, except for a few landmarks that occasionally reared through the oily, gray tentacles of fog. The path before me was now moving upward into sunlit heights. A feeling of warmth was in the air, and the birds had begun to sing in the trees over my head. A bright light seemed to be bathing everything with a translucent ivory radiance. Just when I had determined to take my first step in that upward direction, I awoke with the morning sun streaming full in my face and to the chattering noise of birds outside my window.

Most of my dreams are unfathomable. When I do succeed in retaining the details of a dream in my mind, my abysmal imaginings generally mitigate against any helpful kind of interpretation, so, for the most part, I do not try to make much sense out of dreams. Several dreams, however, stand out for me as sharply definitive signposts, almost to the point of being augural. While this is not a book on dreams or dream interpretation, I would be the last to say that dreams do not often relate to healing and wholeness. Carl Jung has done more perhaps than any other in the field of psychology in linking the basis of our dreams to a religious process. Whether we think of dreams as messages from God or messages from ourselves does not matter too much, I think. The important thing for us to understand is that dreams are just one more signal telling us to look inward for our own reality, instead of projecting our hopes, fears, and wishes onto the outside world.

I have interpreted this dream as a symbolic picture of my life situation. It was showing me that in my life thus far I have fought my way uphill against forces I have viewed as hostile or uncaring. But along the path have been prepared little places of protection, shrines of refuge, where I can stop for rest and assurance. The need for rest is obvious; so is the need for reassurance. We each need to know that it is all right to drop out of life's struggle periodically to recoup and renew, and we each need the feeling of reassurance that the path we have chosen is the right one for us. Yet I have often refused the time necessary to find either rest or reassurance because of my preoccupation with the outer journey. The dream was reminding me that the real struggle of life is an inner one and not an outer one at all. It was telling me to rest for a moment in the love some are giving. It was showing me that the hoary mists are behind me, and though I am not fully out of them, I am in the process of leaving them behind. The frozen misery of my past, where I felt alone and inadequate, is breaking, cracking, beginning to move, and I am now at the point of my existence where I must take the longest stride of soul I have ever taken—exploration into God.

It seems strange to say this, since I have ostensibly been involved in the enterprise of God-exploration since I was first brought into a crude consciousness of God at the age of fifteen. That exploration, however, has never been totally wholehearted in me, anymore than it is in most people I

A Lonely Journey

know. Like a pendulum on a clock, I have swung from an anchorite existence, where I withdrew as a religious recluse of sorts, to the path of a recidivist, who lapsed into former states of loving the world and the things of the world too much. I do not regret any of it. The swinging back and forth has undoubtedly been something I needed to do in order to swing up out of the mists. But it is now time to move forward with wholehearted exploration of my own inner space, which is the equivalent of exploration into God. There can be no more temporizing or acting evasively so as to effect a compromise with God or with myself. There have been many who have loved me and will undoubtedly continue to do so, but at this point in my journey I must leave them and continue on alone. I do not mean that I am removing myself from their lives. Far from it. I could not exist if I did. But the exploration into God, the journey to my inner space, is a journey that I must take alone, just as you must take yours alone. There is much we can offer to one another in the way of comfort, aid, and interpretation, but we cannot take the steps for one another. That we must do for ourselves.

This book is essentially a chronicle of a part of my own interior journey. It is a sharing of some of my thoughts about God and the inner pathways by which I have found God, although it is presumptuous for me to say that I have found God. With St. Gregory of Nyssa I must say, "To find God is to go on seeking him." He is always more than I can know, beyond anything that my finite mind can encompass, larger than any entity my spirit is willing to embrace. Yet I cannot deny his call into the unknown, the incessant call to go a little farther each day, whether down into the darkness of the valley or up onto the lighted peaks. His is a call into solitude, into the stillness of my own being. Since God is dynamic rather than static, as evidenced by his creation, to meet God is to forge ahead into an innermost reality of space that is infinite.

As a child, occasionally fascinated by science fiction, I

found it impossible to hold in my finite mind a concept of infinite space. Now it has become easier. Perhaps I am more in touch with my own infinity than I have ever been previously. Perhaps it is also because my generation has been privileged to live through the inauguration of travel into outer space, one of the most remarkable events in the world's history. When the Apollo spaceship, thrust upward on a pillar of fire, soared into the heavens and landed on the moon, it was the apogee of all human scientific knowledge existing at that time. But that knowledge has continued to grow prodigiously through enthusiastic research and enormous expenditures, until today we know that tourist flights into outer space are entirely conceivable.

Strangely enough these great voyages into outer space have not only heightened our senses of relatedness to the universe, they have also increased our longing for a sense of unity on this earth and a desire for unity within the inner space of our own individual being. Hence, along with the inauguration of the Outer Space Age has come the rise of an Inner Space Age, marked by a great meditation movement. Zen, Yoga, and a form of Yoga, known as Transcendental Meditation, have begun to appeal to people of all ages and in all walks of life. Eastern and Western cultures have met in what some describe as a "meditation boom," but which is really a joint effort to seek interiority in a time when all the boundaries of exteriority are being expanded.

Scientists have become interested in this meditation movement from the standpoint of studying the altered states of consciousness which meditation produces. Though altered states have been around since long before the time of Jesus, science has only recently become interested in them. In one sense this bodes well, for both religion and science have something to contribute to each other. But unless the end result of the combined efforts of religion and science is to produce a higher quality of love and to preserve a humanizing element in a world that grows increasingly impersonal, there is little to be gained from such dialogue.

My concern in this book is not to offer a critique on any particular mode of meditation, either scientifically or religiously. I am simply attempting to detail some of the framework that has been helpful to me in building a scaffolding for my inner journey, as well as to indicate which parts had to be abandoned and why. I am in favor of whatever works to enhance the human potential and to nourish a faith in the Immanent Essence of Life and Love that has brought this cosmos into being and continues to sustain it. I am for anything that will provide an individual with rest and reassurance, for life is a pretty hard prospect for most people. They desperately need to know that there is a way to make it. I am also wise enough to know that what works for one may not work for all, even though the end result will be universally the same.

It may well be the mystic who will lead us into the future, rather than the scientist, and I would simply like to offer in these pages a personal perspective on one way of gaining that mystical path. How to achieve that path is far less important than why it be achieved, for I am convinced until we take that journey into our inner space, we will never satisfactorily conduct any exploration into the outer world. We are created for the inner world, and just as our generation will probably be the last to be imprisoned on this planet earth, so should we prepare ourselves to be no longer trapped in a personal world that deals only with exteriorities.

Certain dangers mark the journey into inner space, which I feel compelled to point out, for the caverns of one's mind and spirit are, in the hyperbole of William Johnston in *Silent Music,* "inner mansions of hypnagogic imagery, unconscious locution, exquisite symbolism and violent upheaval." To avoid these dangers one must determine why the journey is being undertaken in the first place. Is it to explore the subterranean realms of the psychic, or is it to enter into a higher state of consciousness? In my observations the former motive is dangerous and should be avoided. Many people find themselves unable to cope with the images and forces that come to them in the psychic realm unless they are grounded and protected by a strong faith in a loving God. More than one explorer of the inner world has ended up in psychological distress and neurotic disorder because of an inability to handle the temptations and to process the knowledge that came from the psychic realm.

The temptation experiences of Jesus in the wilderness, at the beginning of his public ministry, seem to indicate some of the dangers that exist in the inner life. Following his baptism, he was in the desert forty days and nights without food, according to the Scriptures. The idea of forty here is that of completeness, since numbers in the Bible frequently had metaphysical meanings rather than denoting actual passage of time. This event was undoubtedly an excursion into his own inner being by Jesus in an effort to realize a more complete state of God consciousness. Yet even though his motives were pure, he was tempted by the devil to assume power for himself. He was able to resist the temptations successfully because of his deep centering in God, as indicated by his command, "Begone, Satan! for it is written, 'You shall worship the Lord your God and him only shall you serve' " (Matt. 4:10). At that point the devil left him and angels came and ministered to him.

Through the temptation experience of Jesus we see that one of the primary temptations in the psychic realm is to assume control over the minds of others, to claim power for one's own purposes. Whether we wish to affirm the existence of devils or regard evil entities as the projections of our own interior fears and hatreds seems basically unimportant to me. The important thing is that we recognize the perils of exploring our inner space without sensing first the invitation of God and realizing that it is God who is awakening us and guiding us to infinite possibilities within ourselves. Thus, it is God who initiates the journey and who protects us to its end.

There is yet another peril of the inward journey. One may be snared into seeking the inner world for the sake of the inner world alone and thereby refusing to return to the outer world. If one does not come back from prayer, meditation, and contemplation to the daily routine of life with deeper insights, greater perception, and a refined affection and tenderness for everything, then the inner journey is not complete. Jesus said that his disciples would be known by their fruits, that is, the end product of their lives, their behavior and attitudes, their service. There is always the temptation in the aftermath of a "spiritual high" to want to remain on the mountain and build structures to prolong the experience, as the disciples wanted to do on the mount of transfiguration. But the point of the inner journey is not only to acquaint us with God and with our own spirit, it is also to return us to our outer space less malleable to exterior influences and more genuinely Christ-like to all people and all life. Our goal on earth is to refine our souls as instruments of holy love, and the inner journey is the only way this can be truly accomplished.

We are accustomed to delineating our religious experience as *our* quest for God. Actually it is not we at all who seek God. It is God who seeks us, and our so-called search is but a response to our Creator who has yearned and brooded over us since the day of our creation. God is ever present in our souls. He is present in our dreams. He is present in the deep abyss of our wanderings and in the darkness of our unconsciousness. God is present in us in a manner that makes possible an intimacy with him that would be impossible with anyone else, which is really to say were we to lose a sense of his presence, our inner state would become an icy place of loneliness, a terrifying solitude of utter despair.

Since God is the ultimate ground of our being, our deepest thirst and greatest anxiety is to find him, or to be found by him. Ernesto Cardenal, a modern mystic, has suggested that our coming to earth is a self-imposed exile and that everything we do while here is an attempt to return to the love of God from which we came and for which we are designed. Every human soul reflects this thirst and anxiety for God in various ways, both good and bad. Aberrant behavior is really a response of one's overpowering loneliness for God, for we are all homesick for his love. Every human soul longs to be possessed by a colossal and powerful love and will go to any length possible to find that love and be claimed by it. Every crime committed has as its basic root an inbalance or lack of love, for the human soul is born in love and must spend all its time searching for the object of its love. Even those who murder and maim are doing it in the name of a love that has been denied them or was never fully actualized in their lives.

The ultimate human quest then is not for outer space. It is not for things. It is not for people or a person. The ultimate human quest is for love, a love that is only satisfied when we allow ourselves to be found by God who loves us as no other ever can. The deepest human longing is for God, even though for many that longing has no name. The search for the human spirit, for the kingdom of heaven that Jesus said lives in each of us, and for the inner space where God may be fully embraced by the arms of the soul—this is what we were made for. It is a lonely journey, for God is only truly encountered where all other things and persons vanish. And as have been pointed out, there are certain perils in such a journey. But not to take that journey will produce even greater loneliness and a peril of utmost devastation.

If this book aids anyone in a better understanding or a stronger desire to move forward into the ultimate enterprise—exploration into God—then my purpose in writing it will be achieved.

Chapter 2
Exploration into God

Who is this God toward whom we are powerless to initiate any move of our own souls, but must wait for him to come to us?

To each one of us God means something different. Those differences, however, are not important. What is important is that we recognize *there is God,* call him or it what you will—Creative Principle, Causative Power, Great Constructor, Ground of Being, Heavenly Father, it matters not—and that this God created us. We did not create ourselves. We are created by God and for God, and we are forever in a state of mortal anguish until we start the journey back to God from where we came in the first place.

Meister Eckhart once wrote, "Everything you say of God is wrong." He meant, I think, that essentially there is no way our limited language forms can encompass the allness of God. He is as majestic as the starry heavens and as minute as the digestive system of a tiny flea. He is as resplendent as a desert sunset and as inventively humorous as a snail plodding along under the man-given appellation of *Gastropod Mollusk.* He is as fierce as the force of a hurricane and as quiescent as the three-toed sloth hanging upside down from a tree. Any attempts at comparative descriptions of God only prove that in no way can God be described. He is all activity, all life, all power, and all substance of form that truly exists anywhere.

Journey to Inner Space

I read somewhere that if you can name God or describe his nature, you can be sure that is not God. I think this is true. Most of our belief systems about God have been developed from an overpowering sense of loneliness that impels us to try to describe him so that we may possess him. As long as we recognize the belief systems for what they are and not begin to worship them, we are all right. Once we begin to insist that God is this or God is that, we have trapped ourselves in a dead end that prevents future exploration.

When we are willing to give up all our notions of what God is or is not, we are ready to start the inner journey. Simultaneously, we must give up our human judgments of what is good and what is evil, for as long as we see our universe in dichotomies, we will be forced to see God in dichotomy. We will see God manifested as two powers—a good power and an evil power—waging an eternal conflict within the heart of creation. There is not good God and bad God. There is only God.

One of the great revelations given to us concerning God comes early in the Bible. In the third chapter of Exodus we find Moses in dialogue with God concerning his reluctance to go back to Egypt and deliver his people from bondage. Moses does not feel he has the proper credentials to be a religious leader, and he says to God: "If I come to the people of Israel and say to them, 'The God of your fathers has sent me to you' and they ask me, 'What is his name?' what shall I say to them?" God said to Moses, "I AM WHO I AM." And he said, "Say this to the people of Israel, 'I AM has sent me to you' " (Exod. 3:13-14).

Numerous interpretations have been offered on this passage. Some suggest that God is purposely stressing his inscrutable mysteriousness. Others offer elaborate explanations on the metaphysical meanings of I AM. Extended discussions of these verses soon begin to sound like theological brouhaha, which may then reinforce the notion that God (or the writer of Exodus) was being deliberately obscure. Personally I reject the idea that God wants to hide from us. The entire Bible is a record of God's attempts to reveal himself to his children in as simple a manner as possible and at every step of their life journey. The interpretation, therefore, that comes to me concerning this verse is that God is saying, "I will be who I will be, and in this instance, I choose to be Moses."

Perhaps, then, the I AM is God's name in all those creatures who are willing to make conscious union with God. Perhaps the I AM is the name of our spiritual self, our higher self, our God self, as distinguished from our lower, sensate self. When we are willing to go forth under God's directions, we go forth as the I AM with all the authority conveyed in that declaration. Therefore, the I AM of each individual is the will of God manifesting in its highest aspect, and when we realize that "only through what *I AM* can I serve God," we have taken our first step toward an existential unity with God.

Jesus realized his own true identity was in relationship to God. He saw God not only as the source of his life, he also experienced God as the I AM of his own being. "I and the Father are one," he said, for the I AM of God and the I AM of Jesus had merged into the perfect expression of the Christ. I will discuss this in more detail in the next chapter.

It may well be that the only signpost we will find at the start of our journey into the ultimate enterprise of the soul will be the simple but definitive statement: GOD IS. God is, just as life is. If we start from such a basic assumption, it will offer greater infinite possibilities than if we start from our judgments and opinions about God. From the starting point of God is, we can move to the realization that God is the life of all being, the Creative Principle of all that is. God has made all that is, and all God has made is good. It is then but a short step to the agreement that God is the life, soul, and spirit of you, of me, of each of us.

Unfortunately, much so-called exploration into God never gets anywhere near God at all. It is rather a foray into human evil, human guilt, human poverty, and human disease, with occasional digressions around the periphery of God. My initial introduction to Christianity, when I was an amenable teenager, was at the hands of a sincere but acerbic evangelist whose goal was to expurgate an immoral and scrofulous humanity. Though I responded publicly to his appeal to walk down the aisle and give my heart to Jesus Christ, I felt more bowdlerized than redeemed.

The basic affirmation that God is, eliminates the condition of the antipathetic worlds on which the evangelist had built his case. Nothing is good and nothing is evil, it just is. In the realization that God is will be revealed the potential perfection and harmony of everything. We will not need to labor to change bad people into good people. Rather we shall seek to attain the mind which is in Christ Jesus, to attain the state of spiritual consciousness that he attained, and thus let the good come that already is.

No greater challenge lies before us than this—to look out upon the world with love-filled eyes, to cease judging by appearances, and to realize as we view every man, woman, and child, every situation and condition, that God is. God is in all of his creation, and the spiritual reality of God will be made visible to all when enough people are willing to see it.

The question naturally arises, "How do I do this?" and the answer is, "Through prayer." Prayer is giving over the totality of one's life to the great fact that God is. Prayer is not trying to change God's universe. It is not asking for improvement in God's world. It is not trying to influence the activity of God. Prayer is dropping all personal desires, hopes, and wishes, and moving into the deeper plane of consciousness that God is. All the good for which we could possibly long already is. Prayer is simply the realization that this is so.

I do not find it necessary to differentiate between prayer and meditation, as some do. Though the two may assume different forms initially, prayer usually being verbal while meditation is nonverbal, this distinction quickly disappears if one is really in pursuit of the secret of the inner life. If we will begin by an act of conscious awareness, either stating or contemplating, that God is, eventually we will move to an area of consciousness within ourselves where God begins to function in us, through us, and as us.

I have several friends who participate in Transcendental Meditation, including some who are teachers. They have all told me that this form of meditation does not require a prior belief in a deity, but that no one can practice it very long without evolving a faith in a divine being. To touch the recesses of one's inner being is to touch God. To doubt God is to doubt the validity and infinite worth of one's own being.

The clearest symbolic picture we have in the Bible of God comes from Jesus' parable of the prodigal son, Luke 15:11-32. No matter where the son goes or what he does, the father is still the father. For a time, however, the son chooses to live on finite resources, until he finally discovers he has nothing left. He has cut himself off from the source of his infinity. His inheritance has disappeared. Just as the vine cut from the branch will wither, so the son cut off from the father begins to perish. The son's decision to go back to the father is based on the conscious realization that the father is. If the father will not take him back as a son, perhaps he will take him back as a servant.

The journey back must have been a lonely, heartbreaking one. The son had nothing. He had squandered his inheritance. He had soiled his life and sacrificed his morality. He had only one thought to sustain him, "My father is." It was enough to keep him from dying along the roadside.

What the son did not know, and could not know until his arrival, is that the father is merciful, the father is kind, the father is waiting, waiting for his child to come home, longing and yearning for his return. "While he was yet at a distance," reads the account, "his father saw him and had compassion, and ran and embraced and kissed him." He did not wait for his son to recite his faults or make the proper request for forgiveness. It was enough that he had come home. So Jesus is telling us that the Father God is merciful, the Father God is kind, the Father God is infinite love itself.

Every outer journey we undertake is the result of our inner journey. If the inner journey is shallow, the outer journey will be troubled, for it will lack a depth of resource, it will be cut off from the source of infinity. The realization that "The Father is—God is" is enough to start our feet in a homeward direction. This, the greatest step of your life, can be taken as easily and as naturally as you take your next breath. If you sincerely want to go to God, you can begin by giving sincere voice to this heart-cry: "Father, God, Lord, I am tired of the direction I have been going. I am lonely. I am miserable. I am out of everything. I am even out of myself, and I want to come home." It will not make any difference how you address God, what your theological notions of God may be, or what the condition of your life has been. God, who has been brooding and yearning over you since the rising of your daybreak star, will move to meet you and fold you in the embrace of the most incredible and magnificent love you will ever know.

From thereon the journey becomes successively easier. You are not alone. You are not even responsible. Your only work is to trust God, and your only prayer request will be for grace to know his will and the strength to do it.

As long as we are willing to give ourselves unreservedly to God, God is willing to give himself unreservedly to us. This means we must empty our souls of everything but God. When all the obstacles are removed that separate us from God, and when we are completely detached from things so that we want God more than we want anything else, God will unite himself with us. However, this process of detachment may take time. It is enough for us to know that there is nothing we ever give up to God or lay down in voluntary submission that he will not raise up in an even more glorious form. It is enough for us to know that no matter how beautiful may be the finite, it is tawdry and transitory alongside the beauty of the infinite.

Compare this journey to inner space again to an interplanetary flight. The most difficult part of the outer space journey is at the beginning. Once the spaceship is liberated from the gravity field of the earth, the flight becomes easier, until eventually the pull of gravity from the other planet for which the craft is headed begins to take over. Though the process of detaching ourselves from all but God is a difficult and often slow one at first, if we persist, eventually the soul begins to feel the pull of its true homeland, and the journey grows easier with each passing day.

Loren Eiseley, who for me has been a remarkable blend of the scientist and the mystic, tells of an experience in his youth when he and a friend had trudged all day up a great mountain to a famous astronomical observatory to gaze through the magic glass of the great telescope upon some remote planet. They had no money to join one of the tours organized from the tourist hotels in the valley, but they had an eager interest. However, they were told they could not be accommodated until after the tourists had been served, even though they had arrived before the busloads of people. Eventually they realized they would not be accepted at all, that indeed they were not even welcome on the mountain. Wearily, they began their long, cold descent. In *The Unexpected Universe* Eiseley writes:

> This was my first experience of the commerical side of outer space.... Something was seriously wrong upon that mountain and among the wise men who flourished there. Knowledge, I had learned in the bleak wind by the shut door, was not free, and many to whom that observatory was only a passing curiosity had easier access to it than we who had climbed painfully for many hours.... I remain oppressed by the thought that the venture into space is meaningless unless it coincides with a certain interior expansion, an ever growing universe within, to correspond with the far flight of the galaxies our telescopes follow from without.

Journey to Inner Space

How right he is. It is the inner galaxy that needs our exploration if we are ever to approach the outer galaxies with compassion and understanding. Only in the inward skies can we find the consciousness that will tap the mystery of life and unlock the storehouse to the infinite good, infinite harmony, and infinite wholeness that God has placed here for us. Only those who explore their inner world are given the sensitivity and compassion, when meeting a weary child on the path, to open the doors that will help the child find his way home.

Exploration into God, into self, and into others is all part of the same journey, for to know God, to love God, and to understand God is finally to realize one's own godhood.

Chapter 3
The Way-Shower

Once upon a time a man came to this earth named Jesus. He said he was the Son of God and the way to life abundant and the freedom of truth. He told people if they would follow him they would come to a new life within the realm of what he called the kingdom of God. He went through the cities and villages of the little country of Palestine, talking to people about God's rule in their lives. He performed marvelous and wonderful miracles, such as changing water into wine, giving sight to the blind, cleansing lepers of their infection, making lame people walk, and even bringing dead people back to life. He was followed by thousands, some who were merely curious and who wanted to see him perform miracles and others who came to believe in what he was saying. He gathered around him a small group of disciples to help him in his work and to carry on his message when he was gone.

The little we know today about his life centers mostly around his final three years, during which time he lived exclusively as an itinerant preacher and teacher. Toward the end of those three years, when he was barely more than thirty years of age, he began to recognize that forces were plotting his death. Still he continued his work.

Then one day it happened. The establishment decided he was too exacerbating and dangerous to live; so he was crucified on a cross outside the city of Jerusalem, a manner of execution commonly reserved for criminals of that day.

This man, acclaimed by many to be a prophet of God and the long-awaited Messiah, was put to death because the political and religious authorities feared he was causing insurrection among the common people. He preached freedom, equality, respect for every person. These were dangerous doctrines to give people who were living under subjugation. For that he was killed.

Following his death a most remarkable thing happened. Before any obsequies could be performed for him, his followers claimed that he appeared to them in resurrected, living form, more alive than he had ever been, that he had defeated death and had promised to be with them forever. They went forth as bold, empowered people to establish the worldwide Christian church. They began to put together written accounts of his life, portions of which remain today in translated, redacted forms called the Gospels. They undertook to live their lives as he had lived his and to invite others to do the same.

No one ever stirred up the people of his day as this man Jesus. The greater miracle is that twenty centuries later he is still stirring up people. He was no radical insurrectionist or polemic revolutionary. He was simply a man who knew the laws of God and lived so completely within their framework that his entire life was a litany of obedience and faith to God. He stirred up the people because he showed them what life could really be for them. He continues to do so today.

This Jesus came to be called the Christ, meaning the Anointed One of God. It was a title he neither invited nor disclaimed. Yet what he did was even more startling. He inferred that each person was potentially a Christ. He claimed nothing for himself that he did not claim for his disciples. He called himself the light of the world, and he told his disciples that they too were the light of the world. He said he was one with God and prayed that the disciples would accept their oneness with God. He told them they not only would have experiences similar to his own, but would do even greater things then he had done. Rather than condemning people for their depravity, he sought to awaken them to the glory of their own intended divinity. The task he gave his followers is to realize the Christ within their own consciousness, and to know that the kingdom of God is within them. If they search for it outside themselves, they will never find it.

What went wrong? If this was the salvation for which the world had waited, why did it not work?

The thing that went wrong is that the Way quickly became involved in perfunctory rites and clouded by an atavism reminiscent of early Hebraism. The Christian church developed into an enormous superstructure of hypocrisy marked by ambiguous symbolisms. The large body of Christ-followers failed to realize their own Christhood, and although Christianity claims adherents all around the globe today, the world is far from being Christianized in the deeper meaning of the word. The greatest scandal of the church has been its inability to know the mind of Christ and to inspire others to discover the Christ within. Centuries of christological arguments and flagrant violations of the central ethic of Jesus—love—have produced a divided, fragmented church whose adherents make only hazy, feckless efforts to be truly Christ-like. Many who call themselves Christian set their religious and ethical standards by the Old Testament, ignoring its vast social and theological irrelevance for today, or by Paul the apostle, certainly one of the greatest interpreters of the faith but not the one we are asked to follow.

A religious slogan in our time, popularized by a particular strain of Christianty, is One Way. Another, similar to it, is I Found It. Each refers in theory to Jesus the Christ. However, the more literal and underlying reference is not to Jesus but to a particular opinion of Jesus and a particular version of the Way. I have no disagreement with the right of anyone to interpret the Way and to hold individual opinion of the One who is believed by many to be the Way-Shower. But I disagree with any attempt to try to standardize that opinion as *the only way,* and I deplore the smug assumption of anyone who thinks he has found *it* and therefore has nothing more to seek. God forgive me if I should give that impression in this book.

Each of us must find our own way to the Way, and we would do well to take the hand of the Way-Shower as we go, for he shows us God as no one else ever has. But let us not get lost or overwhelmed by any human forms or formulas that seek to represent the Way. Some of these forms are little more than Jesus cults, stopping short of the Way by worshiping the Way-Shower and dealing almost totally with the miraculous of his life rather than the ethical and the mystical. Let us remember that Jesus came to show us God, to help us share in God's life, and to inspire us to seek the kingdom of God above all else. He resisted all attempts to worship or deify him. Although he did say, "I am the way," he meant that he was the Way-Shower to God. He was not God and never claimed to be.

William Barclay offers this analogy.

> We may direct a person to his destination in words, giving him careful and detailed instructions as to how to get there. We may supply a person with a map which gives him his route and with a careful description of it. But even with the most careful instructions and even with the best of maps a person may still get lost. Best of all is to say to the person: "I know the way, come with me, and I myself will take you there." Then the last possibility of losing the way is gone. For that person we then become the way. Even so Jesus did not only tell us the way; he did not only give instruction about the way; he *is* the way in whom no man can fail to find his way into the presence of God. (*Jesus As They Saw Him* [New York: Harper & Row, 1962], p. 279.)

It is my feeling that Jesus never viewed humanity as innately profligate or immorally diseased. He viewed all humanity as basically good, invested with the potential of Godlikeness and the possibilities of perfection. His invitation was issued universally to every man and every woman to reach for their own potential perfection, which is flawless and eternal. He shut no one out, and he turned no

The Way-Shower

one away. The only people whom he reprimanded were the religionists of his day who burdened the people with self-righteous judgments and tiresome restrictions, rather than freeing them with love and acceptance.

Jesus cannot accurately be considered a social activist. He did not speak out in condemnation against many of the moral evils and social wrongs of his day, for he knew wrongs are never righted through condemnation. His singular condemnation against the Pharisees and scribes bears out the futility of such disputation. They were not converted by his peremptory challenges; they were simply angered to the point of desiring and seeking his death.

By nature Jesus seems to have been an inclusionist rather than an exclusionist. He did not, I think, intend to establish a sect or group apart from and antithetical to other religions. He intended to provide an umbrella that would be an apposition rather than an abrogation to every faith. He came to abolish and destroy nothing, but rather to fulfill everything. He meant to establish a world religion that would embrace every soul and synthesize every creed, and his work will not be consummated until he has done just that.

I regard Jesus as the greatest person who ever lived. He was not only a great teacher, he, more than any other, realized the Christ of his own being and knew who he was in relationship to God. Thus he lived in the most complete love reference to this world that we have ever known. He saw all of life as a drama of redemption with a loving God in search of each soul, not content that even one should be lost. Jesus was the Word of God incarnate in human flesh, the Word who loved its creation and on its natal day pronounced everything good. He continues to inspire men and women today to follow him into the highest way of life, the way of holy, selfless love, and by his abiding spirit is providing us with the grace to receive that love for ourselves and bestow it on others.

I do not wish to advance any polemics concerning the divinity or humanity of Jesus, except to say that I believe implicitly in both. My argument with the Christian church is not that it has made too much of Jesus but that it has not made enough. It has dwelt heavily on his crucifixion and minimized his resurrection. It has preached condemnation to the exclusion of true compassion. It has devised a cult-type of Jesus to be worshiped but overlooked the universal Christ. It has ignored his commandment of unlimited, universal love and has shored up ancient animosities and human judgments with Old Testament and Pauline scriptures. It has encouraged racial prejudice, promoted a myth of fear and hatred around the homosexual, relegated women to an inferior social status, and condoned the easy taking of human lives through war, capital punishment, and other forms of fratricide—all of which are absolute anomalies to the way of Jesus.

If we ever succeed in fully knowing Jesus and fully realizing the Christ in our own lives and living this out in relation to the world, we will see this world transformed at once into the kingdom of heaven. Until then we will go on hating, hurting, and hindering one another in our misguided and uncertain quest for God.

So the question arises, "How can we know him better and follow him more completely?" and again the answer is, "Through prayer." However, we will not find him through the traditional forms and patterns of prayer that most of us have learned. We must seek to understand Jesus' own pattern of prayer and his teachings on the inner life.

I have already suggested that Jesus was not a social activist (in the common definition of that term), nor did he wish to be known as a wonder-worker or miracle-worker. The miracles he performed were the result of his unbridled compassion rather than from any desire to be famous. He had no particular belief or loyalty to institutions and organizations. Jesus was essentially a mystic, a person who explored the deeper recesses of his inner being, found the fountainhead of his own spirit, and thus knew himself to be the Son of God. He began to see the world through

God's eyes; hence he could acknowledge no human hierarchies nor divisions. He saw all things as perfectly whole and unitive in the way God had originally created them, and his goal was to restore all things to that intended perfection. He called people to rise up out of their little selves into a larger life, a larger love, as sons and daughters of the Infinite Father. He saw beneath the sad world of our chaotic construction into the joyous realm of the kingdom of God, and dared to say to everyone, "Come, follow me. I am the way to God."

How did he dare to do this? What madness impelled him to such bold invitations, such cosmic claims?

If madness it was, then it was the madness of one who was inner-motivated and who had learned that when life is lived from *within out,* rather than from *without in,* there are no limits. One can even affirm oneness with God. This kind of madness makes all ideas of sanity appear abstruse by comparison.

The Scriptures allude in numerous places that Jesus had an inner life that he nurtured quietly and privately. He retreated into the hills away from everyone for times of inner refilling, sometimes for as much as a full night. (See Luke 6:12.) He arose before daybreak and sought out a lonely place to pray in order to meet the growing demands being placed on him by the multitudes who were following after him (Mark 1:35). Frequently his prayers were recorded by those disciples who must have been privy to them. Woven into the biblical picture of Jesus was the habit of a man who had learned a rhythm of life, a rhythm of going in to the quiet hours of meditation, prayer, and rest, to be followed by the rhythm of going out to bless and heal human need and mortal hunger.

The disciples observed that when Jesus retreated from them for this inner journey he always returned revitalized and renewed. They noted a fresh power and zeal about him, a calm sense of direction, and a deep inner peace that marked his life with a new quality. One day when he returned from praying, one of them said to him, "Lord, teach us to pray." Jesus began with them by teaching the prayer we know as the Lord's Prayer (Luke 11:1-4; Matt. 6:9-13). He did not mean that the mere repetition of those words would constitute the total act of praying. He only meant it as a beginning, a richly textured framework on which they could build their future explorations into prayer. (A volume much larger than this could be written on this prayer without exhausting its significance and its depth. A later chapter suggests an imagination version of the inception and interpretation of the Lord's Prayer.) It is a great prayer, probably the greatest written prayer the world has known. But Jesus meant it only to be a beginning to the adventure of prayer, a door into the deeper secrets and inner mysteries of a world that is purifying and transforming. He did not intend it to constitute the sum total of our praying, either publicly or privately. In fact, he warned against heaping up empty phrases in our prayers and trying to be heard for our many words. He said the Father knows what we need before we ask him. He also said to "go into your room and shut the door and pray to your Father who is in secret; and your Father who sees in secret will reward you" (Matt. 6:6). Here is the essential factor of his teaching and the mandate for the inner journey that leads to the secret place of one's own individual consciousness.

Notice that Jesus said the Father *sees* in secret. Literally, the Father sees us praying. Nothing is said about hearing. He sees beneath the outer forms of our words to the secret place of our thoughts. He sees our intentions and motives long before they surface into verbal expressions or deeds. He sees into our consciousness, into our hearts. If we will open that secret place to him, which is the purpose of the inner journey, he will cleanse and purify us to a higher consciousness and establish within us his kingdom of love and light.

Our greatest work then is to do no work but only to allow him to do his work in us. He said, "This is the work of God, that you believe in him whom he has sent" (John 6:29).

The Way-Shower

Even our belief and faith in Jesus is God's work in us. The opening of our secret place to God is in and of itself a yielding of ourselves for God to do his work in us. Jesus also said, "Not I, but the Father in me," and, "Before Abraham was, I am." Here is the I AM again. Jesus identifies himself as the eternal manifestation of God, a manifestation, you will recall, that Moses accepted with difficulty and reluctance. Most of us are prone to be like Moses; we cannot believe in our own divinity. But let us not forget that Jesus in his great prayer in John 17 said that essentially the disciple shares in all the riches of the Christhood and in the full manifestation of the I AM. "The glory which thou hast given me I have given to them, that they may be one even as we are one, I in them and thou in me, that they may become perfectly one" (John 17:22-23a).

==This potential oneness with God, which Jesus consecrated as a human possibility, is the goal of the inner journey.== It matters not whether one repeats a word, a koan, a mantra, a scripture verse, or a learned prayer. It is irrelevant whether concentration is focused on one's breathing, the heartbeat, a lighted candle, a mandala, or a cross. It is inconsequential whether the journey involves repetitive movements, dances, lifting up of the hands, the lotus position, the bent knee, or the bowed head. The *how* of the inner journey will always be varied to suit the needs and references of the journeyer. Each must find the way that seems best to him or her. Yet to get lost in the techniques is to miss the journey altogether. What is important is to know that the experience of the inner journey, in its ultimate, is essentially the same experience for all—a sense of oneness with the Infinite and a deep, abiding sense of joy, peace, and love that overflows into all of life. We may choose whatever technique or pathway we like.

It is my belief, however, that if one wants to contemplate truth with a view to becoming one with the truth, he would do well to go to the One who has demonstrated that truth in his own being. Many Christ-like souls have lighted the way in the past, and many are doing so today. But Jesus stands above all of them, "like a lighthouse shining over the dark waters of all our restless seeking." He not only tells us about the Way, he goes with us as the Way-Shower.

Initially I said that the inner journey is a lonely one, that God is only fully realized as all attachments to other persons and things vanish. And while it is true that no human can accompany us to the deepest recesses of our being where God dwells, it is also true that we are not alone in this journey. We have Jesus the Christ. We might phrase his promise, "Lo, I am with you *all the way,* even to the end of the age." I invite you to take the hand of the Way-Shower through every step of your inner journey, for he, more than any other, longs for the transformation of your existence; he, more than any other, yearns for your self-purification; he, more than any other, desires that you discover the fullness and splendor of your own Christhood.

Chapter 4
An Instinct for the Infinite

I sat in a mountain meadow one day, contemplating an army of tiny ants happily climbing up and down slender blades of grass, and asked, "How are we different, you and I?" I wonder if perhaps Dostoevsky might not have also been watching ants scurry hither and yon and was thus impelled to ponder the same question before he arrived at his hypothesis that the ant knows the formula for the ant hill, whereas man does not know his formula. He concludes that the ant arrives here finished and knows what it has come to do, but man is still an unfinished experiment, seeking ever to know and effect his own destiny. From such perspicacious observation are we then to conclude that the ant is the advantaged one, since it is the completed creature and we are not?

It seems apparent, outwardly at least, that animals are satisfied with only the finite, whereas persons can only be truly satisfied with the infinite. To borrow a phrase from Ernesto Cardenal, we humans are born with an instinct for the infinite, an instinct for God, and nothing less than God will satisfy that instinct. Ruben Dario (1867-1916), a Latin American poet, called it the "infinite thirst for the infinitely illusive." It is not so much that God is illusive, I think, as that we conduct our search for him in all the wrong places and in the wrong ways.

The wealthy dowager or the jaded playboy, jetting to the ends of the earth in an irresponsible quest for pleasure, is really in search of God. The tired businessman, who is willing to give a marathon encounter group a try, as well as the suburban housewife, whose longing for personal fulfillment and excitement often drives her to alcohol or an affair, is equally hungry for God. The junkie who "shoots up" and the prostitute who "shacks up" are making desperate attempts to find God. Every face you pass on the street is crying out for God, and every act of lawlessness, promiscuity, and prodigality is an anguished striving for God. The heart of humanity is literally weeping for God, a sorrow compounded by the fact that many do not know why they are unhappy or what it is they feverishly seek. They attach themselves to habits, creatures, and things; yet every finite attachment leads to increased disappointment and frustration because it is not enough.

Dostoevsky said, "Man is not at home with himself, but is, as it were, on a visit." For him the human situation was defined by two factors, imprisonment and hope. We are opposed by a homelessness but sustained by a dream of someday coming home.

In one of Dostoevsky's novels we meet Sonya, the prostitute, and Raskolnikov, the student, who is also a murderer. Raskolnikov senses in Sonya "an inexhaustible sympathy," and he confesses to her that he has murdered an old woman. She weeps for him, as he had wept for her when she confessed the horrible misery of her home which had led her to prostitution. Each senses a great sympathy for the suffering of the other, a suffering far more important than their disgrace or sin.

When Sonya reveals that she prays, Raskolnikov asks her, "So you pray to God a lot, do you, Sonya?" At first she does not answer. Then she whispers, "What would I be without God?" "But what does God do for you in return?" he asks. Sonya hesitates a moment, and confesses, "He does everything!" In God she has met the pure love which does not judge her sin. It enables her to become that love for Raskolnikov, going with him through the confession of his guilt to the police and accompanying him to his imprison-

An Instinct for the Infinite

ment in Siberia. The story closes as together in prison they embrace, sensing that in their love they have found the dawn of a new future and a resurrection into a new life. Dostoevsky shows us that when the unhappy murderer meets Sonya's "inexhaustible sympathy" he meets Sonya's God, and it transforms him into a new man.

The suffering of a burdened humanity is a far greater tragedy than its sin. John W. Bailey wrote in *Life Has Meaning,* "The pain and soul travail, the heartache and dull hunger in those about us would make us weep if we knew." People do not need our judgments or our condemnation; they need our love. Jesus wept when he glimpsed the soul anguish of a humanity crying out for God yet refusing the things of God that would bring peace. He did not condemn; he wept. He knew that the burden of humanity was already imponderably great; it did not need the added weight of his condemnation.

Only in one's deepest soul, alone in the presence of God, can the soul travail, heartache, and dull hunger be healed. Our instinct for the infinite is the same intuitive yearning a hurt child feels at the moment of pain. "If I can just get to Mother or Daddy, it will be all right," so he runs to those arms that hold for him "inexhaustible sympathy" and healing. Our search for God is similar, except we do not always have the wisdom to know that we have a divine parent whose love for us is inexhaustible. We do not always know that it is God we seek above all else, and our search has no name until we discover that our deepest hunger and most pressing need is for God.

Father Ernesto Cardenal, who is in the fore of the renewal of the Catholic Church in Latin America, says that man is on this earth as an exile from God and can only be reunited to God through a true and perfect love. Yet we have no way of making our love true and perfect until we are touched by God's love. His love is a gift given freely to those who will receive it. It is never conditioned by our perfection, for if God waited for us to be good before loving us, he could never love us at all. He loves us as Sonya loved

Raskolnikov, with an inexhaustible sympathy, and that love is ours when we determine to have it.

Yet God gives us more than sympathy. Jesus said, "Blessed are those who mourn, for they shall be comforted." He did not say those who mourn would be given sympathy; he promised comfort. There is a difference. Sympathy means *to feel with*. It can ease one's burden somewhat to know that another feels the burden with him, but more than this is needed. The person who is practically eradicated by grief needs something more than another person wallowing in the grief with him. He needs to have his sadness turned into joy and his fear turned into love.

In my early years in the ministry I was better at offering sympathy than I was at offering comfort. Shortly after I came to my parish in Oakland I was asked to make a call on a woman who was critically ill. She seemed glad to see me and began to describe her condition. In my callow state I thought perhaps it would be good therapy for her, so I listened dutifully and sympathetically. Her conditon had something to do with dehydration of all bodily fluids, which necessitated great liquid intake, eyedrops, and other supplements. She described how raw her throat became without saliva, how gritty and painful her eyes became without moisture. The longer she talked the more I began to take on the symptoms she was describing, until finally I had a raging thirst and a blinding headache. I was genuinely in sympathy with her, but I was not much help.

When I became aware of what I was experiencing, I began to exercise self-control so that this did not continue to happen to me as I encountered sick or needy people. I learned, by God's help, to strengthen my sympathy into comfort. According to its Latin derivative, comfort means *to strengthen greatly*. It comes from two words: *con* (meaning "with") and *fortis* (meaning "strong"). To comfort is to give strength.

God does not merely offer us sympathy; he offers us comfort. It is this gift of his own comfort that enables us to comfort others with a lasting sense of hope. Hear what the apostle Paul had to say about comfort. "Blessed be the God and Father of our Lord Jesus Christ, the Father of mercies and God of all comfort, who comforts us in all our affliction, so that we may be able to comfort those who are in any affliction, with the comfort with which we ourselves are comforted by God" (II Cor. 1:3-4).

The God of *all* comfort, of *all* strength, comforts us in our anguish and affliction and in so doing makes us channels for that comfort (strength) to flow into the world. It is not something we do; it is something we permit him to do in us, through us, and as us.

One of the reasons the human family circle is so important to us is because it is the nearest tangible form of God's comforting love that we have on earth. That is why, as we mature, we marry and establish a continuation or extension of the family. In the wedding ceremony I always remind the couple, "You love each other today because God has loved you always. Try always to understand and see your love as an extension of God's love." If we do not marry, we still reach out to cement ties of love and affection with friends, expanding and solidifying our sense of family even beyond blood ties or legal attachments. Everyone needs a family of some kind, because it partially satisfies the restless yearning and automatic longing each of us has for infinite ties. Those who have no family, no circle of human refuge, where love is inexhaustible, are those who may become violent, lawless, or cruel; or they may move about this earth wearily searching for the experience or person who will supplement the love and comfort that has been denied them.

Yet though the family is the most stabilizing and significant force we have on this earth, and though the family unit in its ideal state is the extension of God's infinite love for his children, it is not enough. We need more. We need more than God's representatives. We need God. As Augustine said, we are forever restless until we find God, or more accurately, allow ourselves to be found by God.

God has made it marvelously simple for us. He is no farther away than our own mind. He is a presence within each of us that is ever seeking to free us from the responses and impulses that keep us earthbound. The first step we take in God's direction is a step he has aroused, and he jealously guards that and all future steps, so that we will finally come to that secret place within, the secret place of the Most High, where our deepest instincts will be satisfied and our greatest potential realized.

Let me not be guilty of making you think this inner journey is so simple that it requires nothing from you. It is, in fact, one of the most challenging journeys you will ever undertake. In the initial stages it is a journey of the mind, and this is what makes it difficult. Few of us are masters of our minds. In fact, it is often humiliating to find how little we are able to control our own thoughts. Once we have managed to keep the mind from racing away from us like some unruly child, the next step is even more difficult, "bringing into captivity every thought to the obedience of Christ." So the first step is to control the thoughts, the next step is to lay aside the thoughts, and not until we can do this can we move into the region within us that is unreachable and untouchable except through the refinement of silence.

We cannot reach God through our minds. Many have tried and failed. We can only reach God in absolute stillness when the mind has been transcended. The mystic who wrote *The Cloud of Unknowing* knew that God is not attained through knowledge or reasoning; God is only attained through that consciousness described as unknowing. This is not a state of ignorance. It is a state of being, where the mind is at rest and the soul fully embraces God. We do almost anything in this world with our minds except reach God.

Though initially I speak about a process of reasoning and a refinement of our intellectual processes that must take place as we begin our journey to inner space, the time will come, if we persist, when the inner journey will cease

An Instinct for the Infinite

to be something we think about; rather it will become a place where we learn to let the mind relax so that God may reach us. Human thought is a heavy mechanism; this is why it is essential that we finally learn to lay it aside. Only then can we enter the place of our inner consciousness where the Immanent Essence of Infinite Life dwells, the very Source for which instinctively we have been looking all our days.

In my enjoyment and appreciation of the natural world, I am constantly amazed that animals know what to do without ever being taught. Not only do they know how to let their own pattern unfold, in their natural state animals rarely suffer stress and they rarely commit suicide. They simply follow their inner instincts to the path of their freedom, unless humans interfere. As Thomas Merton points out, trees and animals have no problem of sanctity and salvation. God makes them what they are without consulting them, and they are content. In fact, they demonstrate by following this path of so-called automatic response that they live freer, more fulfilled lives than we humans do through our intricate patterns of reason and choices. Konrad Lorenz argues, for example, that there is a killer instinct in humans that is often less controlled than in the most savage of animals.

As noted at the beginning of this chapter, we sometimes say that only humans have the instinct for infinity. Some animal behaviorists posit, however, that animals do demonstrate a contact with the Creator of the universe and that no real boundaries separate the human and nonhuman world, except the dark illusion of our senses. I believe this is true. The same creative force is calling *all* life into oneness.

Thomas Merton says, "A tree gives glory to God by being a tree. For in being what God means it to be it is obeying Him. It 'consents,' so to speak, to His creative love. It is expressing an idea which is in God and which is not distinct from the essence of God, and therefore a tree imitates God by being a tree." Are we then to infer that humans imitate God by being human? Yes, if we understand what it means to be human. Our vocation as humans is to work with God as co-creators in our own creation and in the development of the world's destiny. We discover ourselves in discovering God and working with God as partners. Our great burden, however, is the burden of free choice, for unlike the tree, whose instinct for the finite is an automatic force, we humans have the capacity to reject God and to try to be what we are not. Yet the same force dwells in us that dwells in the tree, and the same infinite spark seeks to waken us to be what in God's plan we are meant to be.

Implanted in our nature, therefore, as in all nature, is this instinct for the infinite. If we would give ourselves over to it as singularly as animals give themselves over to their instincts, following it one-pointedly to its Source, we would discover the reality of ourselves and the life for which we are truly meant. This is what Jesus meant when he suggested we consider the lily of the fields as we contemplate our lives, for God has clothed us in such a way that we in our environment are as reflective of his life as the lilies are in theirs. To a racked, unhappy soul this may sound like a mockery. Yet here is the eternal challenge God gives us: Find your peace in me. You will find it nowhere else. And it is planted deep within yourself.

One blustery, cold day as I put on my coat to go out on a busier than usual round of appointments, I looked with longing at my dog curled up warm and cozy in his favorite chair. "Count," I said, more to myself than to him, "today I would like to trade places with you." He opened one eye at the sound of his name, cocked an ear ever so slightly, and gently thumped his tail, clearly refusing my invitation to swap but letting me know that I was welcome to join his world if I really wanted to. As the first blast of driving wind and rain caught me in the face, hurling the open door back against the wall with demonic force, I must confess that I thought my dog had chosen the better part, at least for that day.

An Instinct for the Infinite

Why do we humans drive ourselves with such a febrile pace to such impossible extremes? Surely we are meant to live much more simply, more quietly, more gently, than we do. At the very least we are meant to alternate our pattern of work with frequent and meaningful periods of rest. Often we do not rest when we have the chance, but go tearing off on another furious round of activity under the spurious title of relaxation.

The place of deepest rest and relaxation is at the center of our own being. It is also the place where we receive our best guidance. Many times in the quiet reaches of my own soul I have been clearly told, "Drop this activity. It is taking too much from you, and it is not worth your energy." As I have learned to obey the inner voice, I have also learned that there is an inexhaustible wisdom available for us in the inner space that will help us order our lives to greater peace and fulfillment.

We are creatures with an instinct for the infinite, for the infinite provides us our true freedom, the freedom for which we are truly and eternally made.

Chapter 5
Ceiling Prayers

People have occasionally said to me, "I pray, but my prayers never go any higher than the ceiling." I understand what they are saying, for I have experienced the same thing. In some cases it was because I was toiling under a shadow of darkness that momentarily held me captive. But in most cases it was because my prayers were wrongly motivated and wrongly directed. I was praying for personal gain and personal power to a God wholly transcendent, that is, a God up there, out there, somewhere, or anywhere but within me. I had not yet learned that the best way to reach God is to relax and go into the silence and let him reach me. Consequently, most of my prayers went about as far as the ceiling and no farther.

I think it is basically futile for us to look back on what we were or what we did and deplore any former state. We need every experience we have had to arrive at our present place of realization. But now is the time for us to begin to realize that prayer is not what we say, it is what we are. Prayer is not getting something from God, it is giving ourselves to God. The only goal of prayer must be the attainment of a Christ-consciousness to the end that we may lift the world into a higher dimension of consciousness. As long as we live principally for ourselves and make the fulfillment of our own desires the goal of our prayers we will never reach the kingdom of heaven that

Jesus placed before us as the essential spiritual experience.

If we truly wish to rise from self-consciousness to God-consciousness, we must recognize ceiling prayers for what they are—largely useless and wasted forms that take us partway to the door of the Kingdom but never quite take us inside.

Each person has a human self and a divine self, or an outer self and an inner self. The human self is often contrary to the inner self, for it struggles in a world of opposing personalities and conflicting forces. The goal of prayer is to melt the conflict between these two selves and to put the human self under the dominion of the spiritual self. Many prayers are uttered in great sincerity from the level of the human self, but these prayers are ineffectual and shortsighted, for we are the ones doing the praying. The true goal of prayer is to come to that place where *God prays through us*. Then the great forces that are within us will be loosed on this world to bless and illumine, rather than to be dissipated by irritations, resentments, and fearfulness. Look with me at the various types of prayers that often originate from the human self, the sorts of oblations that usually rise no farther than the ceiling of our own thoughts.

Reverence by Rote

Most of us learn to pray by imitating or memorizing prayers of others. Nothing is wrong with this kind of prayer as a beginning step, but the time comes when we must go beyond rote praying. How many of us would continue to read if we were never offered anything beyond the first-grade primer? Yet we often go on praying in the old forms we learned in our childhood and then wonder why our prayers never seem to make contact.

My mother taught me this prayer when I was a child, and I used it faithfully almost until the time I was in high school:

Journey to Inner Space

> Now I lay me down to sleep,
> I pray the Lord my soul to keep.
> If I should die before I wake,
> I pray the Lord my soul to take.

Sometimes I expanded this prayer into other requests, for this is essentially a prayer of asking. But for many years I did not get far from this concept of reverence by rote. Even when I abandoned the use of a memorized prayer, the prayers I offered spontaneously were often constructed on old patterns of thought repeated in a form that varied externally but not internally. This kind of praying is acceptable for a child, whether physical or spiritual, but it places heavy and peremptory restrictions on our praying, because it keeps us at the child level. The day comes when we should grow up and be ready to move beyond it.

The Lord's Prayer, when prayed in a mechanical, perfunctory fashion can be no more than this kind of rote praying. But there is a difference because the content of the Lord's Prayer offers a depth of spiritual ingredient unparalleled in any other formal prayer that I know. Jesus gave us this prayer as a beginning step into the Kingdom, a foundation on which we would build all our future praying. We never abandon the basic rules and theorems of mathematics. Even in higher math we return over and over to the simple proposition that $2 + 2 = 4$. The Lord's Prayer is similarly the scaffolding on which our prayer life should rest, but it should never be clipped off in a methodical fashion and then labeled as prayer.

There are a number of written prayers that I use periodically in my own quiet times, and when leading in public prayer I usually find it helpful to construct the prayer prior to giving it verbally. This need not eliminate spontaneity nor reliance on the Holy Spirit to pray through us. Those things can occur just as well in preparation as in delivery. Preparing public prayers in advance allows words to be put together in a manner of thoughtful content and beauty of expression that will bless and uplift others, for language is a powerful instrument. This practice also saves us from falling into the use of banalities and monotonous repetitions, the bane of the minister or anyone who does public praying.

I do not mean to infer that spontaneous, unprepared prayers cannot be beautiful. They can be indeed, for it is the Spirit that gives utterance to all our praying if we consecrate those prayers in the Spirit. But prayers, carefully and thoughtfully constructed, can inspire others for many years and can be used profitably in one's inner search. The prayers of the great mystics are some of the most inspired and edifying documents we can read today, and public worship can be truly enhanced by a congregation praying together the great words of a prayer that were forged on the temper of some devout seeker's longing for God. God help us avoid that anathema of true prayer, reverence by rote. Otherwise we are little better than the Pharisees of Jesus' time who smote their breasts and raised their voices on street corners as they prayed in order to be seen and praised. "Truly," said Jesus, "I say to you, they have received their reward" (Matt. 6:5). Reverence by rote carries its own reward, but beyond a mild state of euphoria and a pleasant sense of duty done, it offers little else.

Appeasement by Anguish

There is a kind of praying that takes its rise from a false concept of God. If prayer is viewed as an attempt to appease an angry, vindictive God, what greater way to appease such a God than to grovel in visceral anguish? Occasional evidences appear in the psalms that the writers may have been trying to pacify an angry God by the impassioned fervor of their prayers. I do not mean to paint all of the psalms with one stroke of the brush, for some of them are magnificent and remarkable examples of prayer at deep center. The book of psalms, however, is a Jewish prayer book composed by a number of different people over a long period of time. As such it reflects various cultural situations and national crises, as well as theologies developed on various levels of spiritual search. Some of the psalms advance a picture of a stern, judgmental God, quite different from the picture of the loving parent that Jesus presents, whereas other psalms move ahead into a realm of truth that is both timeless and universal. The fact remains that prayer built on the premise that God must somehow be placated is ceiling prayer.

Although Jesus said that the penitential prayer of the publican ("God, be merciful to me a sinner!" Luke 18:13*b*) was a more acceptable prayer than that of the Pharisee who noisily gave thanks for being better than others, he did not mean that penitence should be the sum total of our praying. We all have genuine moments of anguish when the only prayers we can manage are desperate cries for help, but we can be sure that we do not need to pretend remorse or parade penitence. We *have* his help the very moment we are willing to declare honestly that we need it. He is a God of unlimited love with complete compassion for our wrongdoings and mistakes. He wants to remove anything that separates us from him and bring us into our destined inheritance as holy sons and daughters, and this is exactly what he begins to do the moment we allow it.

How vividly I remember Miss Ada chiding young Keith Sutton for engaging in fisticuffs at the Sunday school picnic and suggesting to him that he ought to tell God he was sorry. Keith squinted both eyes tightly shut and confessed heroically, "I'm sorry, God, but, by gosh, I'll bet if you had to be around Jimmy Snodgrass all the time, you'd give him more than a bloody nose." There is something admirable in such honesty, but someday Keith must learn that God has to be around all of us all the time. No one is left out, because he is a part of all. The amazing thing is that it is not God who deals out the bloody noses. We do. God is forever trying to renew us in his love and trying to heal our minds from the centuries' old view that he is punitive and vindictive. We can share our anguish with him in the absolute confidence that he understands it far better than we ourselves do and that he cares for us in our suffering beyond human degree or comparison. But there is nothing about God's nature that demands appeasement, for God neither punishes nor rewards. He is simply trying to appear on this earth as us.

Injury by Intercession

Praying for another is the highest gift we can offer, for true prayer is formed in the consciousness of pure love. What a tragedy that we misuse prayer as a weapon against people, either as a way to get them to bend to our will or to coerce them, through divine control, into our image of what they should be.

Nearly twenty years of radio ministry have brought me into contact with people of many different theological persuasions. Frequently, when I have disturbed someone's doctrinal fortress, I have received letters pointing out my heresies and directing me sternly to repent of them. Usually these letters end with this final threat, "I'm going to pray for you."

The fact is that we are never qualified to pray for anyone as long as we are using prayer to bring a person into line with what we think that person should be. We do not have sufficient wisdom to choose another's path of thought or action. The only thing we can safely do for another is to lift up the Christhood in him or her and let our judgments and preconceived notions of right or wrong fall away.

I once knew an old woman who demonstrated this style of punitive prayer by "letting 'em have it with Psalm 109." If one takes the outer meaning of Psalm 109 only and applies it strictly in an external way, it is a harsh and dreadful curse leveled against someone who has been evil or hateful, not terribly different from the primitive rites of voodoo that seek destruction of a person. I personally believe there is another way to view this psalm in application to one's inner life, but even if it is an ancient prayer against an enemy, it is a serious misuse of prayer.

Intercessory prayer is not making people over in our image. Real intercession, at its deepest level, always frees us to allow others to be what they are, as well as what they are not. Even if you have part of the truth, you must learn that you cannot hit people over the head with it.

Dialing for Devotion

In far too many instances God is treated less courteously than we would treat a friend whom we call on the telephone. With the friend we usually allow and expect some reply and interchange. With God we often do not. We call him, tell him what we have to say, and then hang up before God has an opportunity to say anything. Not only does this deny the basic ingredient of prayer—God's time to communicate his will to us—it also treats God as a servant doing our will. There is no such thing as God doing our will. Just as we cannot appease God by being outwardly anguished, neither can we influence God by our much speaking, for he will never be the servant of our will.

Prayer is meant to be an opening of our consciousness to God to the end that we may become receptive to his grace and his will. How may we expect to experience his grace or to know his will if we fill all our prayers with chatter? God does not need our words; he sees what is in our hearts and reads our thoughts before words are ever formed. The value in verbalized prayer is for the pray-er to see where his thoughts are leading. The words become a reflection of the inner state of consciousness. What God wants most from us when we pray is our receptivity, our willingness to listen to him, to bring our total being under his control by stilling all noise within and without. He has a glorious destiny to reveal to us, but it is utterly impossible for him to communicate that destiny as long as we are trying to tell him what destiny we would like.

Let us not become discouraged if we are not immediately successful in sensing God communicating with us. After all, we are trying to break a lifetime habit, and it may take us sometime before we are able to feel God is speaking to us. The fruit of learning to listen in the silence is that sooner or later God will say to us, as he did to the older brother in the parable of the prodigal son, "Son [daughter], you are always with me, and all that is mine is yours." That will be the beginning of God's impartations to us whereby even our human mind becomes his mind. Once we have stood at the periphery of that experience, we will never again return to our former methods of calling God and then hanging up before he has the opportunity to speak.

Hiding in Holistics

A wise man once said, "Behold the turtle, he only makes progress when he sticks his neck out." By contrast, note the ostrich, the largest of all birds, whose extreme timidity often leads it to bury its head in the sand. Some people use prayer as an escape from dealing with the world.

A young mother once confessed to me that her greatest frustration when she tried to have a morning quiet time was that her children would not leave her alone. They seemed to choose that time particularly to bother her with their requests and needs. Since there was little way to change the children's schedule, I suggested she change her own and choose a different time, perhaps when they were asleep. We are fortunate if we can build our prayer schedule to suit our own whims, but few of us live in such a way that we do not have to take into account the lives and needs of others. We should not attempt to, for to be oblivious to the humans who share this world with us would indicate a gross insensitivity and disregard on our part. After all, the inner journey is not for our benefit alone; ultimately the world profits by every person who realizes the God-consciousness.

The Christian way is the servant way, and whoever seeks divine light must be prepared to be a channel of light for the world. Moreoever, we will discover as we learn to go into the silence and listen for the still, small voice that instructions will often come to us of things God wants us to do: people to see, tasks to do, causes to support, and the like. Anyone who settles for the ostrich approach to prayer and avoids the assignment of servanthood will discover that his prayers are not even reaching the ceiling. In fact, they are reduced to the size of a prayer rug and will do little good for anyone, including the pray-er.

There are undoubtedly at least a dozen more examples of ceiling prayers. It should be sufficient for us to know that prayer is not an exercise where we beseech and bewail, any more than it is an opportunity for us to give God information and instructions. Any forms that lend themselves to these directions are essentially unproductive and futile. Attaining that mind "which was also in Christ Jesus," which is also to attain our Christhood, is the primary purpose of the journey to inner space. Whatever comes as a result, whether to us or to others, will always be beneficial, but the results are only secondary and should never be sought for themselves. Jesus said if we would first seek the kingdom of God, meaning if we would give first priority to the journey within where that Kingdom is found, then everything we need will come to us. There is a point in this journey where we cease to be the traveler altogether. We cease to be the doer. Instead we become the instrument on which God performs his mighty works. That will happen as we learn to move beyond the ceiling of our thoughts into the higher dimensions of God-consciousness.

Chapter 6
Freedom Through Surrender

On several occasions I have made the polar flight from western United States to London. It is always amazing for me to realize as I soar above the Arctic seas dotted with icebergs that only three-tenths of each floe is visible with the remaining seven-tenths submergd beneath the water. Here is an analogy of the fundament of our lives. The greatest portion of our being is in the world of the invisible, the world of our inner life, with the visible being nothing but the out-picturing of that vast, invisible world.

This truth is the heart of the greatest sermon humanity has been given, the Sermon on the Mount, where Jesus Christ teaches us that outer things are but the result of what happens on the inner level. Murder is the result of angry thoughts, adultery the result of lustful longings, divorce the result of spiritual disharmony, and so forth. Jesus was trying to demonstrate that problems of moral behavior cannot be solved by changing the outer rules; people's hearts must be changed. This entire treatise, which is the essence of Jesus-Christ-faith, is to help us evolve from a preoccupation with the outer world (the Law) to a concern for the inner world (the Kingdom). His promise is that if we will seek the inner world first and give it our highest priority, we will be given everything else that we need or want.

The invisible is the only reality. Until we understand that basic premise, we are captives in a prison of ignorance, heaping destruction on our earth through the venting of hypocritical judgments and malicious attitudes. This planet is a schoolroom where we must learn to realize the invisible while we are in the visible, to experience the incarnation of God in our corporeality, and thus to express spiritual ideals through the forms of flesh and blood.

We dwell in a sea of negatives. The outer world is rampant with hatred, prejudices, violences, fears, disorganization, greed. These things are the result of centuries of wrong thought forms, and they often cause us to give way to the despairing belief that ours is an alien, hostile universe where most things work against us. This is not so. The evils of this world comprise only three-tenths of it at best. Great forces of inestimable good lie buried beneath the surface of the visible, waiting to be brought forth from beneath the frozen waters of material life by those daring, intrepid souls who are willing to venture far enough beneath the surface to release them. One lone person overcoming a difficulty in the outer world by prayer—which is an experience of the inner world—is helping the entire human race, past, present, and future. The good that surfaces through a single life making its act of religious devotion is greater than the evil that comes forth from a thousand sinful lives, for good is the greatest force in the universe. It is always self-multiplying, whereas evil carries within it the seeds of its own decay. That is why we call Jesus the Savior. He surmounted within himself every limitation humanity might encounter, including death, and offered to each soul a saving path for its own inner overcoming.

But the path that leads to the fullness of life is also a path that encompasses death. Every man or woman who sets out to make the journey into his or her inner space must be prepared to die totally to self before a true identity can be encountered, for one's true identity is not in the personal ego but in God. The ego is the three-tenths of our being that dwells in the visible world. In the invisible world the ego can only exist if it is surrendered, totally and without reservation, to God.

Let me define what I mean by ego, for the term can be misleading and confusing. Psychology considers the ego to be the superficial conscious part of the id, which is the concealed, inaccessible part of the psyche, developed in response to the physical and social environment. Philosophy uses the ego to mean the entire person, body and mind. In metaphysics, ego comes to mean the permanent real being to whom all the conscious states and attributes belong. It is from the latter definition I am working. The ego in and of itself is nothing. It has been described by Charles Fillmore as "a mere ignorant child of innocence floating about in the mind of being but through the door of its consciousness must pass all the treasures of God."

Metaphysicians often differentiate between the adverse ego and the spiritual ego. These are opposite states of consciousness, the adverse ego manifesting itself when it becomes attached to sense forms, such as material greed and selfishness, and the spiritual ego manifesting itself as the individual center of God-consciousness. There are not two egos; only one, expressing itself in different ways. The spiritual ego would then be the true self, or as described earlier, the inner self.

The term ego had not been invented when Jesus was teaching. He often used the word life when referring to self and said that to lose one's life (self) for his sake was to find it. Today he might well say that to lose one's ego in God is truly to find it. The goal of the inner journey is not to negate the self but to bring about its true freedom. The journey is designed to take us from self-consciousness to God-consciousness, from self-centeredness to God centeredness, from self-imprisonment to self-freedom.

Though the inner path is one that leads to freedom, that freedom is paradoxically accomplished only through surrender. Though it leads to life, that life only springs forth when one is willing to die. No real sense of personal identity can come until one is willing to give all hope of identity into the hands of God, for just as one part of us is always seeking the freedom to know ourselves and to be ourselves, another part of us is always seeking for someone or something to which we can surrender the self that we call ours.

Here then is the purpose of the inner journey—to discover the persons we are and to place these into the hands of God, to be emptied of all desire to exercise personal self-will in favor of God's will, to be willing to set aside anything and everything (even our opinions) to find and know God.

Many people in this world suffer from wounded and deflated egos. They have been made to feel that they are no good, of no value to anyone, worthless. These people need to have the ego strengthened and emphasized, and for them modern psychology is a much-needed help. Many others suffer from inflated, oversized ego. Everything they do centers around themselves. The principle word in their vocabulary is "I." These people do not need to be given any techniques for strengthening the ego. They are insufferable enough as it is.

Jesus offers us a greater possibility. He says that we should lose the ego (self) by offering it to a force greater than itself. He counsels us to surrender the ego to God, to lose our lives in God so that we may truly find them and thereby find our destined freedom. Every person is designed for total freedom. No one is meant to be enslaved to anyone or anything except to God. Our voluntary enslavement to God saves us from a weak and failing human way and sets us free to be our highest and fullest selves.

Someone has described the surrendered ego as being so much *not there* that something greater than the ego can be seen. This was the way of Jesus. When people saw him, they saw God. Through Jesus' surrendered self God visited this earth as he had never done before and has never done since. The promise is that we all become heirs of everything God has given to Jesus as we learn to surrender the ego.

A personal illustration might demonstrate this point further. I have never truly aspired to be a public speaker. I have felt sincerely called by God to speak, but I never set out to build my own platform or to seek prominence as a speaker. Although I have been invited to speak at retreats and camps in numerous states and several foreign countries, and although I speak daily on the radio to an audience estimated in the tens of thousands, this particular part of my life has never been anything I have designed or necessarily wanted. In fact, I am still surprised that it is so, for though I work harder at speaking than anything else I do, no activity leaves me feeling more nervous and inadequate.

I have finally learned a secret, however, and that is the secret of being "not there" when I prepare and when I speak. With my full being I try to empty myself in order that God may have control of me, both in preparation and delivery. My prayer becomes an empty cup, lifted to God for the filling. I have discovered when I do this that my emptiness becomes my freedom, for I am not depending on myself and my limited abilities. I am depending on God and all his infinite resources.

I have also learned that we are never immune from the peril of spiritual pride. Once we do something well we usually begin to think that *we* did it, that *we* really are good at doing the things we do. There is a sense in which *we* did do it; there is also a sense in which any significant work of permanent value is never performed by us but by the Father who works in us and through us in the same manner he worked in Jesus. (See John 10:37-38; 14:10-12.) Should several persons tell me that I am the best speaker they have ever heard, and should I succumb to the temptation of believing such flattering nonsense, I begin to lose my freedom. I am imprisoned again in the web of believing that I do not need God, that I am totally adequate for all things. When this happens, I accept for myself the praise that really belongs to God. This is the great deception. No matter how good we are, we are never *that* good. In and of ourselves we are, in fact, neither adequate nor good. Some vital, living quality is missing when we begin to think we are. The point at which we are so much in the way that God can neither be seen nor heard in us is the point at which we begin to fail.

I heard a plump, homely girl sing one Sunday morning in a little country church. She accompanied herself on a guitar. Her voice was clear but untrained. She pronounced some of her words poorly, and the song she sang was exceedingly simple. There was no extraordinary display of musical skill. Yet few singers have moved me as she did. Something happened when she sang that I always look for but rarely see in the performance of the most polished vocalists. For a little while she stepped completely aside and let us see God. Her singing was a total self-offering instead of self-seeking or a self-taking. She sought neither attention nor applause; in fact, she was simply not there at all, and she lifted all of us into a sense of God's presence. It would certainly enrich worship if there were fewer performances of the ego and more opportunities for God.

I do not mean to impugn singers as the only examples of the adverse ego; I only use them to point to the dangers we all face. God has blessed each of us with special gifts and unique talents. He gave these to us so we could use them, both to his glory and to our own sense of satisfaction. But only as we learn to give these gifts back to him are we really free in using them. Otherwise our gifts rule us and become hindrances to our intended freedom.

Freedom is the largess of God, given as liberally to all his children as it was given to Jesus. Jesus Christ is the paradigm of the one who found freedom through surrender and who demonstrates to us that the bounty of true freedom comes only to those who consciously and consistently surrender everything, even the possibilities of freedom, to God. We can never surrender everything at once, for our resistance is too deep. We can only give what we can when we can, until little by little our resistance is worn down through every effort. Our greatest work ultimately is to do no work; our greatest effort is to cease striving and straining and come to that state of total abandonment where we discard every form of self-rule and self-effort in favor of God-rule. Yet God is no capricious despot; he is a benevolent parent whose wish is to set his children free—free to rule their appetites instead of being ruled by them, free to take their rightful place of dominion in the outer world instead of being dominated by it, free to embrace the entire universe in love instead of withdrawing from it in fear, free to release all feverish efforts and frantic strivings in favor of one supreme effort: letting God do it.

There is nothing new about any of this. Brother Lawrence in the seventeenth century said, "When we are faithful to keep ourselves in his holy presence . . . it also begets in us a holy freedom . . . wherewith we ask . . . the graces we stand in need of." There is even a step beyond that, which is to arrive at the path of desirelessness where we want nothing and ask for nothing because indeed we know we have everything. Now *that's* freedom!

The journey to inner space takes us to the eye of the storm and into a quiescent stillness where the soul is nourished, the mind enlivened, and the body empowered. This is so we may return to our outer space, illumined for both our tasks and pleasures and wonderfully free to be our truest selves.

Chapter 7
The Greater Love

Love is not only the highest commandment of the Christian faith, it is the supreme law of the universe. We are told in the Bible that we must love God with the fullness of our being and our neighbors as ourselves. Jesus identified this as the greatest law and added a new dimension to it when he said that we should love one another as he loved us. Whenever we try to break this commandment of love, we end up breaking ourselves, for it is the innate law of our being.

Absolutely nothing on this earth that we do is more imperative than fulfilling the divine law of love. The first step in fulfillment is lifting love from the materialistic, sensory viewpoint of the visible world and understanding it as the predominant activity governing the invisible world. This invisible world, defined by Jesus as the kingdom within, is the place where God reigns supreme. Jesus tells us that God is love, and if we would become God-like and assume our individual Christhood, we must love as God loves.

Many people limit their concept of love to filial affections or sexual activity. These, however, are only manifestations of human attachments that are destined to dissolve with time. They are at best but dim reflections of the greater love that is basic to God. If we participate in the greater love, known by the Greeks as *agape,* it will certainly purify and ennoble our human affections and

The Greater Love

activities toward mate, families, and neighbors, but these human bonds are not necessarily synonymous with the love that is associated with God. In fact, human love void of divine love tends to be restricting, frustrating, and painful. Human love is at its highest when divine love is the controlling ingredient. By this I mean our love will always be faulty and inadequate until we learn to love in the manner in which God loves us.

How does God love us? God sees and knows everything as good, for God is the Creator who has invested infinite good in all he has created. Scripture tells us that God is not judging us according to our sins; he is showing us mercy. God does not care for us less because we are imperfectly expressing our divine nature, for he sees us as we are destined to become, rather than as we are at any particular moment. We would not love a little child less because he or she thinks poorly, speaks incorrectly, or does not have full physical coordination. We recognize these as aspects of the child's future development which have nothing whatsoever to do with whether or not we can love the child. This is the manner in which God loves us. He loves us as saints becoming. He is not impatient with us because we are not yet full grown. He is not condemning us for past errors or mistakes of judgment. He is not despising us because we have failed to live up to our highest potential or because we have chosen to squander our spiritual inheritance in a country far from our Source. Through all we do or fail to do God is loving us, loving us for all the innate strengths we possess which will yet come forth as an expression of our potential perfection, loving us as holy sons and daughters becoming. God is loving us because he sees the good, the goodness in us.

It is this gift of greater love that enables us to see the good that is inherent in everything, to see God in everything, to see the potential perfection in everything. Greater love is the ability to look out on the world and confidently assert, "God is. The perfection of God *is* in me, in others, in all." Granted that each of us still has a distance to go before perfection fully manifests itself. For some the way is longer and fraught with more difficulties than it is for others. Those who have experienced enlightenment need to give gentle yet powerful support to the brothers and sisters who are struggling under tremendous burdens. No one is any better than another; some have just moved a little farther along the path. We need to recognize that what we call wrongdoing is simply the Christ in that person calling out for help to one who is in the light. We must be merciful, not judgmental, considerate, not condemning, for this is the way of the greater love that sees the good in all and feels in harmony with all.

If we persist conscientiously and diligently in pusuit of the inner space, eventually a new state of greater love will develop within us. We will begin to live and move and have our being in God. We will relax all sense of living our own lives and allow the larger life to live us. God will act in and through the spiritual temples of our consciousness, appearing in this world as us and enfolding us in such total oneness that divine love will flow through the channels of our lives to bless and heal the world.

That quiet center where "I in God" and "God in me" are one is the most freeing experience we can ever have. No longer need we feel separated and alone, limited by our own knowledge or conditions of birth or bound by our judgments and dislikes, for we will find ourselves plunged into the stream of an infinite love that satisfies us at the level of our deepest thirst and flows through us to merge us with all life. When we make contact with God, the Source of life, we make contact with everything that God has created, and we become one with all of creation. This is the ultimate of the inner journey—total oneness with everything, which is the result of our complete absorption into the greater love that has created all life and sustained it through its aeons of struggle. God is patiently bringing everyone and everything to its intended destiny of glory and fulfillment. Greater love teaches us to trust a process we cannot always see.

We must not try to separate love into human and divine areas and to concentrate on one to the neglect of the other. Greater love unites all other loves, and whoever learns to love God fully learns at the same time to love man as a brother and woman as a sister. The gift of greater love, coming from the Father-Mother God, enables us to see God in every person and to see every person in God.

Obviously something is wrong in the world. Things have not turned out as they were intended originally. Something profligate, disordered, fearfully evil in our world keeps back the flow of greater love. There is a tragic version of history that cannot be overlooked. Hitler slaughtering Jews and Hiroshima destroyed by the atomic bomb are but the explosions of poisonous effluviums and polluting exhalations that have been corrupting humanity since the day Cain slew his brother Abel. A pestilential malignancy has spread its disease over the face of this earth and left populations starving, uprooted, immured, debased, and despairing. This is not a theological treatise on the origins of evil, and if it were, I could not explain *why* sin has happened. The *how* of sin is more easily explained. People have turned from God and have said no to the greater love that God offers. But why? We cannot understand it. It is a baffling thing that people will continue to do the very thing that inflicts such terrible suffering on everyone, to turn from the reality that makes for their peace.

Yet though we cannot understand it, we must nevertheless accept things as they are and start now, step by step, to return to the promised land of our own being. We must retrace the path to the Source of the greater love and let it guide us to the building of a new humanity and the shaping of a new world. The pure and eternal love of God, which waits for all who puncture the outer wrappings of life and move to its deepest center, will draw us up to the higher way of treating one another as in our essential being we want to be treated. At its inception this love is deceptively simple, because it starts within our own hearts and moves from us in a concentric pattern, touching first the mortals who share our daily life before it sets off the ripples that eventually are felt by the world.

I was leading a prayer group one time at a religious retreat held in the mountains. In that group of about ten persons was a middle-aged woman and a young girl who were exact opposites in terms of life-styles, temperaments, and mannerisms. Charlotte, the woman, was attractively groomed, severely reserved, and devoutly religious. Margo, the girl, was hippie-like in dress and language and bubbling over in her openness and energetic sharings. She seemed driven by a boisterous need to foster the attention of the group, whereas Charlotte was quiet to the point of being withdrawn. As the week progressed these two persons worked an adverse effect on each other. Charlotte's facial expressions indicated silent disapproval of Margo's vociferous domineering, and this seemed to stimulate the girl to drag forth more and more of her past history of lurid sexual promiscuities and drug experimentation, observing Charlotte's face as she spoke for any possible shock effect.

I felt that Margo was crying out for acceptance from us, that her boastful recitations were more confessional than chauvinistic, but acceptance seemed to be the last thing Charlotte was capable of extending. Then she adopted another pose. When Margo began to talk, Charlotte opened her Bible and began to read, clearly indicating that she had erased the girl. I do not know how she managed to do it, especially if she read anything like the Sermon on the Mount, but she did, at least outwardly.

One day as I invited the group to go into the quiet time together, I watched those two persons and prayed silently for a reconciliation to come before we dispersed. Charlotte sat in her chair, stiff, upright, rigid, her face locked and frozen. Margo, quiet at last, sprawled on the grass, her head huddled in her arms as she hugged her knees. They were only a few feet apart physically but miles apart in every other way, and that distance was complicated by the wall of mutual resistance each had helped erect.

Then a sweet, grandmotherly little lady in the group began to speak. "It has come to me," she said in a gentle but firm tone, "that God has chosen each of the members of this group to be together for a very special reason, and that each of us is a kind of human laboratory where the others must come to learn. We are helping one another see our own individual faults. If one of you stirs me to impatience, it is I who must deal with the problem, for it is I who am at fault. I want to thank Margo for helping me see some things in my life that needed to be corrected. She has been for me a special gift from God this week."

I looked at that beautiful old soul, sitting there with eyes closed and hands folded serenely, and wondered how any unkind thought or evil intent could ever cloud her vision, for she was outwardly one of the most loving persons in the entire group.

Then a man spoke. "Margo has blessed me. She has helped me feel a compassion for my own daughter, who left home a year ago because I didn't give her any freedom to be herself. I'm going back to find my daughter and see if we can start over."

One by one the people in the group spoke affirmingly of Margo, lifting up her strengths, expressing their gratitude for her. It was an amazing experience. They had been able to look beneath the visible exterior of Margo to the invisible reality of her soul.

Margo was weeping now, muffled, choking sounds escaping from her bowed head.

And then the greatest miracle of all took place. Charlotte stood up. For a moment I feared she was leaving, but she moved toward Margo. Crouching in the grass beside her, she drew her into her arms. I heard her utter two words as she buried her face against the girl's hair, "Forgive me." Margo clutched her like a soul drowning, and Charlotte rocked her gently in her arms while tears steamed down her cheeks and ruined her makeup.

A peace of indescribable dimensions descended on our group, enshrining that moment as forever hallowed for all of us. It was a moment of seeing God, a moment when the inner journey had brought all of us to the interiority of one another, breaking down every barrier of resistance and recrimination that had existed among us. The glorious onslaught of God's greater love in our midst refined and purified our imperfect human love and lifted it to the higher dimension. It brought us into a communion where the symbolic bread and wine elements of our Lord's presence were the flesh and blood forms of his followers.

The Lord's Supper, as Jesus meant for us to observe it, is a feast of greater love. The Upper Room, that he prepared and made ready for his final meal with the disciples in Jerusalem, is still prepared for us today. But it must be more than a ritual observance conducted periodically at a formal church service; it is essentially a place within our own being, within the vast room of our inner space, where he invites us to come and feast with him. Before we enter this chamber, we must lay aside the garments of the outer world—tired, stained attitudes and dusty habits, vain preoccupations and fears, overnurtured likes and dislikes—in order to come into the holy of holies as free and unencumbered as it is possible for us to be. There at the altar of our own consciousness in the upper room that he has prepared, we are reminded of his words, "If you are offering your gift at the altar, and there remember that your brother [sister] has something against you, leave your gift there before the altar and go; first be reconciled to your brother [sister], and then come and offer your gift" (Matt. 5:23-24). Into that upper room of our inner space we must therefore bring every man, woman, and child of our acquaintance and let his holy love purify our love toward the creatures with whom we share the outer space. "Do this in remembrance of me" are the words of institution for Holy Communion. In prayer we are remembering our way

The Greater Love

out from limiting earthbound thought forms into the divine freedom of a Christ-filled life.

Consider for a moment one symptom of an estranged relationship, anger. Anger is a normal, predictable reaction that every creature experiences in a world not fully redeemed but struggling to realize its perfection. To repress or deny anger is unhealthy from both a physical and emotional standpoint. To express anger to the one who has made us angry is a better way, for it relieves the inner pressure that accumulated anger creates. The thing wrong with this method is that it may make the one expressing anger feel better, but it leaves destruction and havoc in the pathway of others who may not really deserve it. Often the ones toward whom we choose to express our anger may not be the real target at all but just the ones who happen to get in our way.

There is a better way to handle anger, transmute it into love. This can be most effectively accomplished in prayer and meditation, where human will is placed in total subjection to divine will and where every human emotion is offered up for cleansing and transforming. Confess the anger to the Holy One. Agree that you do not wish to carry it any longer. It matters not whether you are the innocent victim or not. Lift up the person or situation that has angered you to the highest realization of which you are capable by enumerating all the good qualities, potential and actual, that are there. Ask God to bless that person or event with his light and love and at the same time to transmute your anger into sympathetic understanding. If you stay with it in a sincere belief that your anger can be directed into constructive channels for the common benefit of all and that God has the power to do this, you will gradually sense a great peace invading your heart that will completely replace your anger. Remember that you do not have full knowledge. You do not know why certain persons are as they are. If you knew, it would only enhance your capacity to forgive. God knows. Trust God to do in you and through you what you are not able to do for yourself.

Trust God, who has bestowed the nature of holy love in all creation, to bring that love forth in you, that it may reach forth in communion with the hidden splendor that is in everyone and everything.

Occasionally our deepest angers are unrecognized, blunted by the familiarity of being with us for long years. I spent much of my early life nurturing an anger against my father because he did not, from my perception, fulfill his obligations in the father role. I looked on him with contempt because of his weakness with alcohol and resented the fact that I had no father as did most of the other children I knew, since he and my mother were divorced when I was two years old and he was therefore largely absent from my life.

Fortunately, that anger was wiped away and healed forever when my father died. When I saw him in his coffin, I had the greatest sense of love for him I had ever experienced, for I suddenly realized how hard and lonely his life had been. He did not need a single moment of my anger, he needed my understanding and my love. The day I exculpated my father was the day I began to discover him, to appreciate his strengths, to be grateful that I was his son. There are times now when he is strongly with me as a gentle, encouraging presence, and every memory I hold of him is hallowed by the greater love of the heavenly Father who is actively restoring the lost and wasted years between an earthly father and his son.

If I learned any one thing from this experience, it is the necessity of laying aside all my opinions of what is good or bad. I have no way of judging anything, because what I classify as good or bad is merely my human evaluation of it. I am sure God is unaware of one person being good and another bad, for God is not limited to such mortal opinions. God sees beyond the manifestations of our humanhood into the divine being that is really ours. Therefore, let us not waste time praying to God to make bad people good. It will not work. It has been tried for thousands of years. God is absolute, unmerited, unlimited love, and we must come

The Greater Love

into conscious oneness with God to become the outlet of that love. We cannot do that if we are categorizing people into saintly and sinful clasifications. Our work is not to pray for God to punish or redeem a scurrilous humanity. Our work is to turn within for a realization of the presence of God, and then to see that out-pictured in our own experience and in the experience of those around us. Real prayer is the purest form of love that exists, and this love ultimately takes in the world, for it is free of judgments and restrictions.

We have the choice of either being ruled by the events of our world or ruling them. We are not victims of anything unless we choose to be. We are destined to be victors. We are created to rule our own world. But to rule wisely, nonjudgmentally and with absolute regard and love, so that the outer events are transformed, is a task that will at best be ephemeral and transitory until we learn to let the greater love completely control us.

In olden days of warfare there was an explosive device used for making breaches in walls known as a petard. Love is the petard that breaks down the walls of our imperfect lives and helps us discover one another in the larger plan of creation. In the contemplative silence of our own inner being that petard is built and hurled at the outer world, leveling all the defenses that have prevented cosmification, and leading us into a love affair with the universe for which all creation has been straining and striving.

Chapter 8
Let There Be Light

The Creation story, which is recorded in Genesis, tells us in the opening verses that God created light before he created the sun and the earth. We say this is scientifically impossible, for there could be no light without the sun. Although the Creation story makes no claim to be scientific, it is not impossible at all, for we know today that light is a form of energy and that all living things are made of this energy.

There is a cosmic light in our solar system that is released from the sun and accumulated in the atmosphere. Existence, as we know it on this earth, would be impossible without that cosmic light. There is also a cosmic light at the center of our being, which is a self-luminous intelligent substance that causes a certain vibratory action in the universe, and this light is the constructive activity and divine wisdom of God producing harmony and peace. Without this spiritual light we would perish as surely as our bodies would die if taken from the physical light of the sun.

So God first made light as spiritual energy and from that light created all things. We, therefore, are not made of solid, impenetrable matter—we are made of light energy. This primal force of energy is what we call God. When the Bible says we are made in God's image, it means that we are constructed of the very energy force which is God. When we establish a connection with God, we receive an increased flow of this energy. This light energy, which maintains and sustains all creation, vibrates at too high an intensity and too fine a wave length for the human eye to see, yet it is more powerful than the rays of the sun. While we may not see it, we can feel it, and when it is strongest in us, we often sense it as a kind of tingling heat that revitalizes and reenergizes our entire being.

When people advance into the higher realms of spiritual consciousness, they often perceive this light through the spiritual senses, sometimes diffused into brilliant colors that go beyond any shades and hues ever seen before, just as they will often distinguish sounds that normally the human ear cannot register, because they vibrate at too high an intensity and too fine a wave length. The deep center of our inner space, where we are conscious of being filled by God, transcends all mortal limitations and brings perceptions to us that are impossible at any other level.

For centuries it was known in the Eastern countries that a powerful, invisible force seemed to flow through the hands and arms of the so-called holy people. People who consciously identified with God seemed to have an abundance of energy which was healing in its effect. Certainly this was true of Jesus. When Jesus laid his hands on the sick, he was able to heal them of their diseases and infirmities by the powerful, vibrational flow of light energy that came through him. Today, as we are beginning to recognize this flow scientifically, we are standing at the edge of understanding his healing miracles as well as apprehending the literal truth of our own being. We are in deed and fact the very healing light of this world. If we ever succeed in fully tapping into that flow, we will perform miracles of healing even greater than those which Jesus performed.

We can never receive this intensified light into our beings, however, until we seek it at its source, God. This light is God, manifesting within our lives as the active, life energy. As we study to adjust and conform ourselves to the laws under which that light operates, we will be able to receive it and send it forth as the highest blessing we can offer to this world.

Our greatest life goal ought then to be to dwell in the light rather than in the darkness, for this light is the miracle-worker. When we are illumined by the light from within, we are in touch with our Source, and we will always have as much of the light as we are willing to transmit. We lose it if we seek it simply for ourselves. We are meant to be the vessels through which God sends his light into the world to replenish and to restore the broken areas of creation where the light has become dim or deficient. In the process of transmission, we, the transmitters, are renewed.

Let us no longer think of this light in a purely symbolic sense, as we have been prone to do for centuries. I am talking about a spiritual reality that is more real than the sun which lights and warms this earth. A few mystics of the past, including Jesus, knew that a cosmic light dwells at the center of our being, projected to us from beyond. Unlike scientific light, this cosmic light is neither static nor still. Rather it is an impelling force, which, if sufficiently released, could take charge of this wayward earth and bring it back to its original goal. While this light is projected from etheric realms beyond this earth, it is also at the center of every person's being, and as more and more persons realize this fundamental fact of their existence and learn to release the light, it takes command and moves all creation forward to its highest possible achievements. It pushes all discord back to its source, causing it to return to the Creator for redemption.

Most students of the spiritual realm agree that we are entering today into a New Age of Light on this planet. This light is beginning to expose and correct malfunctions in the created order. The result of this may be a temporary increase of distress and disease. Individuals who have been dwelling in darkness will manifest hostile and criminal reactions as the light increases. There will even be similar disturbances in the elements of nature in the form of storms, droughts, earthquakes, and other destructive activities. Humanity as a whole may react to these upheavals with feelings of despair and doom, fearing that the world is coming to an end, as limited thought forms erroneously predicted long ago. But this is not an age to fear, it is one in which to rejoice. As the light purges and purifies the darkness, we feel the death rattle of an old age and the birth pangs of a new one in which the highest aspirations and possibilities of creation will rise to the fore.

Those who understand the principle of light, who know how to project it into a condition and hold it there, and who understand that this light comes from God and God's invisible workers who are on this earth, will discover that they are able to change conditions in positive ways and usher in the age of abiding peace on earth. This light is to our spiritual activity what blood is to the physical body. It is the light that allows us to accept all things in a nonresistant manner. When we are fully clothed in this light, we draw to us that which is our own, and nothing else can touch us. We are completely protected. As we learn to release the light consciously, it moves forth from us as a constructive activity, holding supreme authority over all darkness. These light currents radiate out from us just as a bulb radiates its own kind of illumination.

This light was released upon the earth on creation day, but subsequent centuries of human self-seeking and sin dimmed its force. A few great souls, such as the mystics and prophets, managed to keep alive a vision of that light returning to shine upon the earth inhabitants who had been dwelling in darkness. Isaiah, in the eighth century B.C., described this light to his people as that which would multiply and increase their joy, would lift the burdens of oppression from their shoulders, and would initiate a reign of peace to which there would be no end.

The light was redelivered to the earth two thousand years ago through Jesus Christ as the activity of life, the radiance of life, and the substance of life, with power to restore to us the divine authority that had been all but lost during the long period of darkness. How clearly the writer of John's Gospel described the coming of this light in the prologue to his book: "In Him was life, and the life was the light of men. The light shines in the darkness, and the darkness has not overcome it. . . . The true light that enlightens every man was coming into the world" (John 1:4-5, 9).

Jesus delivered the Christ-light of the cosmos to the planet earth and to each of us individually, and in our own age we are finally beginning to see the promise of its fulfillment that Isaiah described long ago.

Little wonder, then, that the birth of this amazing Jesus to a peasant family in a tiny, remote country was surrounded by supernatural manifestations of light, such as the appearance of angels and a star. Nor should we be surprised that as the Child grew to adulthood, his path was illumined by continuing experiences of light, climaxed by that moment on a mountaintop where he retreated with three of his disciples to pray and meditate, where the light was manifested so powerfully that it transformed him until he shone brighter than the sun. Later, after his crucifixion, when the women went to the tomb where he had been buried, they had an encounter with the light when a being, whose "appearance was like lightning, and his raiment white as snow," said to them, "He is not here; for he has risen, as he said" (Matt. 28:3,6).

As we examine the scriptural records, we begin to perceive the reliability of his claim, "I am the light of the world." He literally walked in the light. But can we also accept his statement to us, "You are the light of the world"? Jesus never claimed anything for himself that he did not claim for us. We are through him the Christ-light on this earth in human form today through which God touches his world. We are part of God, and God's life within us in the form of light energy is ready to blaze forth as the

Let There Be Light

transforming miracle, if we will walk in the way Jesus walked before us.

The Renaissance thinkers said that man, the microcosm, contains the universe, the macrocosm. And so we do. Perhaps that is the uniqueness of our human ability—we alone of all creatures can contain more than ourselves.

As a child I sometimes imagined that the night sky was actually a vast, black curtain spread over the earth, and that the points of light called stars were little holes in the curtain through which light streamed from the heavens beyond. Moreover, I imagined that the continual shining of the heavenly light on that curtain would eventually wear the holes larger and larger, a fact well attested since some lights in the sky were brighter than others, and that eventually the curtain would become so thin it would disappear. Then the earth would have eternal light. My childish fantasies were motivated, I suppose, by the fact that daytime was a more appealing time than night, since the latter called for an end to all games and activities that I cherished then.

I see now where my fantasies were not symbolically wrong. Each of us is, in fact, a truth-hole or light-opening into the great universal mind, through which the light of God is ever trying to pour in order to illumine human consciousness. Some minds are only tiny pinholes, while others are fair-sized apertures. The only curtain that separates us from heaven and the great light of God is the curtain of our mortal minds. This is a self-created separation that came about long ago because people turned their backs to the light and began to live with a darkened sense of self.

But today many are waking to the truth that there is no need to dwell in the shadows, and they have faced about and are receiving the light. They are partaking of all the blessings of that light for themselves, while at the same time they are blessing the world with an illumination of the Christ. These, who have learned that there is no separation between them and God as long as they do not turn away from the light, are responsible for the dawning of the New Age of Light.

Once we decide to face the light, our decision will be constantly tested. We may meet creatures so nefarious in their deeds that they will arouse a profound sense of outrage in us. Only as we learn to bring them into the light with us, refusing to let them violate the essence of our inner being and refusing to damage them further by our judgments, will we be able to help them and eventually find the place of holy protection where we are all safe. We cannot dwell in the light and harbor negative criticisms and judgments of others. Likewise, we cannot dwell in the light if adverse egotism or desire for power or attention dominate our actions. God only gives the light to those who are willing to be the transparencies through which the light can perform its own healing works. God only gives the light to those willing to be the instruments and the servants through which the light may shine.

Can you not see then why there had to be a Jesus? God was as much in the world before Jesus as he was after the resurrection. But there had to be a Jesus through whom the Christ-light could shine before others could stand still and face the light for themselves. There had to be a Jesus before others could see the power of a fully surrendered, nonresistant life. When Jesus walked this earth, there were still disasters and diseases of incredible magnitude. It was impossible for him to permeate the entire world with peace and harmony, because even with his high degree of spiritual consciousness he could not bless and help those who were not willing to receive help. The light will not shine in the lives of any until it is invited to do so. Jesus could not force peace on those who did not want it and on those who would not consciously seek it. But when Jesus appeared, the God-consciousness had a pure channel through which it could flow into this world, and the way was opened for the light to make its entrance into your heart and mine.

The great plan is for each of us to contain the Christ-

Let There Be Light

light. Our highest goal is to let the light come into our lives with all its power to transform and to bless. We will then find it possible to send it forth to others. *Seeing others in the light* is a way of prayer that will help restore the divine image that may be broken in them. It will also be possible for us to surround ourselves, our homes, our automobiles, our loved ones, and all things in a shining band of the Christ-light for invincible and perfect protection. Is it too difficult to believe that God wants us to be safe while we are on this earth pilgrimage and that he has made available all the resources for our safety if we will but claim them?

This is not to say that we will avoid all darkness once we begin to claim light. Our walk on this earth must ever be an alternating experience between the light on the mountains and the darkness in the valleys. All of this would indeed be most confusing were it not for the simple fact that the better of the two, which is light, is the thing we are made for and the thing which will ultimately prevail. We are made for the light, but we need to spend some time in the darkness in order to realize the light and to claim our divine inheritance. I believe for all of us there will come a time, if we are persistent and conscientious in attending to the journey of our inner space, when we will live forever on the peaks, fully bathed in the light. Until that day arrives, we move on with the sustaining belief that God is simultaneously light and darkness; or to put it differently, God is the creator of both light and dark and is present in each. Though we must experience darkness in order to reach light, we can be comforted by the fact that we are never alone. "Even though I walk through the valley of the shadow of death, I fear no evil; for thou art with me." This is enough to keep us going.

It was after midnight when I stood on the deck of my study in the Oakland hills above the cities that rim the San Francisco Bay, contemplating the Christmas Eve service that was just over and seeking some moments of quiet before I turned my attention to the final polishing of a sermon that I would deliver at our Christmas Day worship. The lights below me sparkled like jewels in the clear night air, and a cold breeze sweeping up from the bay caused me to draw my jacket closer. Then the chimes on the tower of the church at the foot of the hill began to play Christmas carols, sending out the timeworn but ever-fresh message of God's love in Jesus Christ.

> Yet in thy dark streets shineth
> The everlasting light;
> The hopes and fears of all the years
> Are met in thee tonight.

As I listened, superimposed on that carillon of music, came the strident, opposing scream of a police siren. I watched a car racing along the freeway below at high speed, weaving in and out through the sparse traffic at that hour. Not far behind it was a police car, siren blaring and red light blazing, in hot pursuit.

There it is, I thought, the picture of the human struggle. Against the backdrop of God's call for peace, the children of darkness continue their struggle, hurting themselves and others, until they learn that it is for them the light shines, it is for them the Savior comes.

Always there will be these sounds in conflict—the siren and the chime—until enough of us have claimed the light and send it forth to shine so powerfully in the darkness that the darkness cannot overcome it. The ancient commandment of God rings out above the rubble and chaos of our saturnine milieu. Let there be light! Let go of your darkness, and let come the light!

Chapter 9
The Meditation Experience

Practically everything that has been said up to this point has been a philosophical discussion of the inner journey as seen from a personal viewpoint. It is now time to turn from theological discursiveness about the journey and present some travel tips that the reader may find useful. In this chapter I offer a brief compendium of the more popular types of meditation, most of which have invaded Western culture rather recently, and conclude by sharing the techniques of my own method of prayer-meditation as a possible path to one's inner space. I underscore again meditation is an individual affair, and each must follow his or her guidance and direction in choosing the procedure that leads to the desired place of higher consciousness.

Although I do not distinguish between prayer and meditation in my private use, certain distinctions are historically and pragmatically noticeable. The path of ordinary prayer invokes or seeks the help of God in fulfilling one's chosen desires or needs, whereas meditation is the path to desirelessness, generally requiring that the devotee sacrifice personal desires with a view toward union with God, or some superpersonal goal. Prayer usually affirms traditional values as the content of divine will, whereas meditation seeks a transvaluation of all traditions. Prayer in its initial stages is usually confessional in an attempt to achieve self-purification, since the need for Christian prayer is predicated on human sinfulness and the necessity of forgiveness. Most meditative disciplines posit no such view of human depravity, at least as the motivational factor for meditating, but rather contemplate truth with a view to becoming one with that truth. It is perhaps an overstatement to say that prayer is always active and meditation is always passive, yet such distinctions often hold, except in the case of contemplative prayer which becomes passively attentive.

Since I have already devoted an earlier chapter to traditional uses of Christian prayer, which from my perception are largely noneffective, let me pass over the subject of prayer and discuss briefly some of the main techniques of meditation before I offer my own formula for blending prayer and meditation into reification within the Christian reference.

Buddhist Meditation (Zen)

In Zen the student is instructed to count his breaths from one to ten and repeat. If the count is lost, he returns to one and begins again. After he is able to concentrate completely on his breaths, the student then begins a more advanced exercise of focusing attention on the process of breathing itself. This involves thinking about the movement of the air within the body, the air reaching the nose, going into the lungs, and going out again. Since breathing is a repetitious, rhythmic activity that continues whether we will it or not, it is believed that this is the most convenient way to begin to get in touch with one's innerness.

While meditating, the student is instructed to remain motionless with hands folded, eyes open, and legs crossed in the lotus position, the latter being something that most Westerners can only manage with difficulty and some not at all. When I studied Zen, we were allowed to sit upright on chairs with backs unsupported if we could not manage to fold our legs for half an hour or more without intense pain. But I was somehow made to feel I would never reach

The Meditation Experience

the high peaks if I was not able to sit in the lotus position. Perhaps that is why I never progressed far toward enlightenment in Zen.

After the student can successfully maintain awareness of his breaths, he is given a riddle or a paradox, called a *koan*, to meditate on. This is a compelling method of forcing intense concentration on a single thought and is not to be taken logically. It is simply an exercise in concentration designed to smash the reasoning process.

Advanced Zen is carried on with a Zen master. The goal is *satori*, an abrupt alteration of awareness or consciousness synonymous with enlightenment.

Yoga

Yoga is a Hindu system of abstract meditation that involves withdrawal from the world and is much more varied than Zen. The goal is the same—alteration of consciousness—but concentrative meditation is only part of the activity. Meditation is directed toward an object with the purpose of identifying one's consciousness with the object. As one advances, attempts are made to alter basic involuntary physiological processes, such as blood flow, heart rate, digestive activity, muscular activity, breathing, through concentration.

In most Yoga meditation practices a *mantra* is used. *Mantras* are words of religious significance, such as names of the deity, which are repeated over and over, either aloud or silently. The focus of attention on the *mantra* is similar to the Zen focus on breathing. *Mantras* are both chanted aloud in groups and used individually. Silent use is also permissible. An example of a *mantra* is *om*, which in Hindiusm represents the name of the Supreme Being.

I participated with a group of college youth once at a religious retreat where we sat in a circle around a campfire with arms linked and chanted *om* for nearly half an hour. After losing my initial feelings of self-consciousness and wondering what my deacons would say if they could see me, I began to feel myself drawn slowly into a consciousness of complete and utter unity and self-forgetfulness. Time temporarily lost its significance, and I felt merged into past, present, and future dimensions simultaneously. God seemed somehow very near through the group chanting of that primitive name. I do not mean to say that I arrived at *inka,* the peak-point where I could avow, "This is it!" I am not sure that is any such point on the mystical path. Surely there is always something more that lures us on in the quest of enlightenment or religious ecstasy, so that one summit only points to another. But in any event, that experience of chanting *om* around a campfire in the Sierra Mountains drew me into a sense of relationship with everything I could perceive—the people, the fire, the mountains, the stars, the divine other—and left me both unified and detached at the same time.

Various forms of Yoga involve visual meditation techniques of sitting in a lotus position and viewing a *mandala,* a specially constructed image, or a stone, a vase, a candle, a rose. Sometimes awareness will be directed to the audible input of a sound, either imaginary or natural. Or the student will be directed to create visual images within, such as a lake seen from a mountain, the earth seen from a distance. In these cases the *mandala* or the objects are used for the same purpose as the *mantra.*

Occasionally the *mudra* will be used. This involves repetitive physical movements, usually of the arms, legs, or fingers. Awareness is directed toward the movement, a simple one being to touch the thumb to the other four fingers repetitively. The *mudra* may also be combined with a *mantra.*

Transcendental Meditation

Transcendental meditation is a form of Yoga which has become popular in the United States. A specific *mantra* is given privately to the student who repeats it silently over and over for about half an hour twice a day, once in the morning and again in the evening. No special posture is required; rather the student is encouraged to be comfortable. Any thoughts which arise are dismissed as insignificant with all awareness being concentrated on the *mantra*. I am less personally familiar with TM than the two previous forms, although I have read *The Science of Being and Art of Living,* by Maharishi Mahesh Yogi, the bearded, flower-decked Hindu monk who established Transcendental Meditation in India, Europe, and the United States. I believe that it could give fuller and deeper meaning to any religion if pursued conscientiously. While the techniques may vary, the end goal is essentially the same in TM as in other mystical traditions. Possibly TM lays greater emphasis on the transformed society than do some traditions whose major emphasis is on the me.

Sufism

Sufis are mystics usually associated with the Muslim religion. It is more difficult to obtain information on Sufic practice, for manuals are not easily available as they are in Yoga and Zen. Sufis believe that techniques must be administered personally, since what may be helpful to one may not be helpful to another. Sufis are bound by no religious dogma, and much Sufic practice is unknown outside of traditional inner circles. They believe Sufism to be the secret teaching behind all religions and are therefore at home in all religions, even though they are often designated as an Islamic sect.

I have had no experience with Sufism except to appreciate its religious poetry and to admire the whirling dervishes, an order that performs spinning dances which, when combined with repetition of phrases, result in trances and ecstatic visions. Again we see the combination of physical movement with sounds corresponding to certain forms of Yoga. Sufis would say this simply results from the fact that theirs is the basic teaching within all religions.

It would not be fair to leave this brief survey without pointing out that similar forms of meditative practices also exist in Western religions, including Christianity. The contemplative life has always been present in Christianity, although it has never captured the masses. Jakob Boehme, a German mystic who lived from 1575 to 1624, used to practice fixing his gaze on a spot of sunlight on a cobbler's crystal as his object of contemplation. He was a Christian, but he was using a form of Yoga. St. John of the Cross gave instructions for spiritual exercises that were akin to Yoga *sutras;* so did St. Ignatius of Loyola. Many prayers in both Judaism and liturgical Christianity are repetitive chants ("Hail, Mary, full of grace"), not much different from Hindu *mantras*. In a Pentecostal service I once observed people moaning and swaying with eyes shut and hands clasped, while they intoned over and over, "Jesus! Jesus! Jesus!" And in nearly every Christian church in the world, no matter how unadorned it may be, can be found the cross, an object to contemplate during worship, just as in every Jewish synagogue can be found the star of David, each one a *mandala,* in a restricted sense.

The problem with any technique for altering consciousness is that it can become automatic and ritualistic, thereby losing its original purpose and meaning. The process is less important than the state evoked, and we should never feel ourselves locked into any one system so that we begin to worship the system instead of God who is above all systems. Neither should we become rigid in one particular pattern of meditation and fail to allow for the invasion of new techniques and changes. If you place the control of your quiet time into God's hands, it may take some surprising turns.

Any technique we might discuss has existed for centuries, for human beings are essentially alike in many ways. We have the same type of nervous system, whether we be a Buddhist master, a Tibetan monk, a Hindu adept, or a Baptist minister. It is not surprising, therefore, that similar techniques have evolved in religious practices as we explore the path to the spiritual realm and make human attempts to reach God. Since the search is really initiated by God, who is always in search of us, it is even more understandable that we do similar things as we respond to that holy questing, and when we arrive at the peak experiences and states of altered consciousness, it is essentially the same experience for all, regardless of what we call it or how we get there.

The advantages of meditation as a means of preventing stress disorders are well known today, since it produces such major body changes as a slowing of breath and heart rate, decrease in oxygen consumption, lowering or stabilization of blood pressure, and decrease in skin conductivity. Scientific research is now indicating that regular meditative practices lead to a maintenance of physical health beyond the average state, produce a state of relaxation deeper than that achieved during sleep, and can be an effective means of stress alleviation. Those interested in further pursuit of meditation as a regenerative process should read Kenneth R. Pelletier's excellent book, *Mind As Healer, Mind As Slayer*. Research evidence in this book indicates that meditators are more psychologically and autonomically stable as well as less anxious, and while meditation is not a panacea to replace all other aspects of life, it does have positive effects on an individual's entire existence, no matter what philosophical belief system it accompanies. The purpose of my discussion, however, is to show how meditation helps us know God and respond to God's will for our lives. Any physical unstressing that accompanies the meditative process is a benefit but not, in my opinion, the major reason for meditating.

A Personal Sharing

Anytime is a good time for turning to God. I find morning is the best time for my own prayer-meditation, since this enables me to start the day in a tranquil, serene mood and helps me meet the day's challenges and distractions with greater equanimity and composure. Also, I am usually in a better listening state in the morning than at any other time of day, since I am rested and refreshed.

I always sit in the same chair if possible, which faces east. Facing east while praying is an ancient practice which draws a symbolism between the rising sun and the dawning of divine light in one's consciousness. In the opinion of some this also offers exposure to greater forms of cosmic energy.

I first read from the Bible or some devotional material that will help me realize the presence of God. I set no time limit on this reading, but it is usually not less than ten minutes. I purposely select reading that will provide my mind with content for the meditation period.

When I have finished reading, I sit erect, both feet flat on the floor, hands open in my lap in the receiving position. The position is important. It should not be necessary to move during the meditation time. In fact, the body should be so much "not there" that it literally asks nothing from us during the period of meditation. Crossed legs, slumped spine, folded arms, or any slouched, careless position restricts circulation and prevents receiving the flow of the Spirit into our bodies.

I usually do a few simple exercises of rolling my head in complete circles, several times in both directions. I also find it helpful to tense my neck muscles and draw my head down between my shoulders like a turtle going into a shell, the releasing it suddenly. It is also helpful sometimes to stretch the arms and move them out from the body in a windmill motion. After I feel physically relaxed and comfortable, I sit quietly and begin to concentrate on my breathing. I take a number of deep breaths, exhaling them slowly. This process is extremely energizing and healthy for the body and should be done often. As I breathe, I concentrate on receiving the energy of God as I inhale and discharging any toxic poisons or pollutions from my system as I exhale. The length of these physical exercises depends on how long it takes to direct conscious relaxation to my body, an important preliminary to the meditative state. Sometimes I vary the procedure and do the physical toning of my body before I read, for if the body is both relaxed and alert at the same time, so is the mind.

Then I close my eyes and begin to focus on God, letting God flood my being with love, peace, and joy. A simple affirmation, usually spoken, such as, "God, I am here, and you are here," helps bring me into alignment with him. Any vocal prayer I might offer during this time is to God but not for God. God "sees" my prayers. He reads my thoughts before they are ever expressed and sees the deepest intents of my heart. Vocalization is for me. It reorders my subconscious center into a holy state of spiritual receptivity. At this point I may slowly pray the Lord's Prayer, the Twenty-third Psalm, or some other psalm or prayer of the higher consciousness, concentrating on the deeper meaning of the words as I say them.

Then I begin silently recalling any thing that came to me from the earlier reading. I have made it a practice to carry at least one truth with me from the printed page into the meditative state, for this process moves the concept from the intellectual or mental state to the spiritual and emotional plane where I can begin to use it. I dwell on the concept or concepts as long as may be necessary, perhaps repeating them audibly as I continue to breathe the breath of God slowly and deeply.

At this point I may offer any other vocal prayer that I feel would be helpful. This may be where I make confession for some wrong, give thanks for particular blessings or benefits, as well as go through a mental list of people whom I hold up to God for his blessing, while offering myself as a channel for his love to flow into their lives. I do not follow any rigid, ritualistic pattern, but rather I let happen what will. On some occasions I spend nearly the whole time in gratitude; occasionally I linger longer over my confessions, for the Holy Spirit is using that time to cleanse me and teach me forgiveness; and now and then I find that most of the time is spent as an intercessor for those whose names are sent to me by God.

During all this time I sustain a strong feeling of God's nearness and guiding presence, immersing myself deeply in his great love-energy and channeling this out to all the world. I am letting God use me in the way he wishes. I am his instrument, surrendered as completely as it is possible for me to be at that moment. It is in the deep silence of my own being that I can freely use the term "Father" when I think of God. Feminists are trying to eradicate the use of any term for God that denotes the male image, and in order to avoid disputation and to be more lovingly inclusive, I attempt to avoid masculine references to God in public prayer. But in my own soul I have reserved "Father" as the term by which I address God, for the intimacy and endearment that this word expresses is practically unparalleled for me. Therefore, when the curtains are drawn and I am in my own holy of holies, God is my Father and I am his little child, loved by him as I am by no one else. So powerful is that love that often I do nothing but sit in the awareness of it, letting it roll over me and surge through me. Sometimes there are tears, sometimes there is inexpressible elation, generally there is a strong, abiding peace. No meditation experience is exactly like another at its center, even though the incipient steps may be both similar and endemic. There comes a point when the Father takes over, and I am no longer in charge. This is the point at which I have sufficiently emptied myself as to let his word be my word, his thoughts my thoughts, his life my life. I can never force this to happen, but it usually comes in varying degrees of intensity if I am regular in the practice of meditation. More often than not it is manifested as a quiet sense of peace and contentment that permeates my total being; the powerful, intense emotions are more the exception than the norm for me, although I have experienced both.

It is normally at this point that I begin to receive what I

call "my lesson for the day." A stream of thought begins to unfold in my consciousness that I have learned to recognize as the Father's word. It is nearly always personal, occasionally corrective, and ever gentle and loving. Here God speaks to me about myself, helping me see where I need to change, affirming my gifts and talents, reassuring me of his love, giving me guidance where it is needed, and blessing me with such grace that I feel as the ancients must have felt when they "found favor with the Lord." I have not yet received instruction for anyone else unless it is in regard to my relationship to another person, pointing out ways that I need to be more loving and less judgmental. The materials shared at the conclusion of this book in the section called "Water from Deep Wells" are samplings of what has come to me through my meditations during the period of time I was writing this book.

It is important to lay the groundwork carefully in this matter of receiving so that all the channels are clear. Otherwise, what might be interpreted as the wisdom of God is only the confusion of personal wishes coming forth from our own complex mental system. It is also important *not* to seek this experience of receiving for the sake of the experience itself. God must always be sought for God and not for his gifts. We receive different gifts in proportion to our individual needs and capacities, and we should never expect to have the same inner experience in meditation that someone else is having. Some form of divine wisdom and guidance is always available for the earnest seeker, but the forms and channels through which these come may vary.

When no specific guidance comes, I continue to sit quietly and seek the still point, sometimes using visualization methods. I know that if I continue to listen intently to him in the silence, he will give me his love, joy, peace, and other fruits of the Spirit, charging and recharging me as a new creature in Christ. Always I must make conscious effort to surrender my total self to the Father that he may do with me, in me, and through me what he wishes. This is especially important on those days when I felt recalcitrant and rebellious, for my life can soon be darkened by opacity if I do not keep steadily facing the light. After I have been in the silence for fifteen or twenty minutes, resting in the sense of being loved and cherished, I usually close my meditation by giving thanks for my blessings and for any small increases of conscious awareness that may have come to me. I breathe deeply several times and open my eyes. This reentry to the conscious level from the superconscious, where I have experienced harmony with the divine mind of the Creator, must be accomplished slowly so that I can transfer the glow of his presence to the conscious, physical plane where I shall be functioning for the rest of the day.

The meditation is now completed in one sense; in another it is just beginning. The experiences within the silence are validated by how well we are able to use in our daily walk the instructions and gifts that have come to us in the silences. God does not share himself with us so that we may hoard and store the experience for our own benefit; he gives himself to us so that we may live more effectively, love more totally, and bless more completely. Otherwise prayer and meditation are little more than the cult of the realized me. The Christ who appears to us in our silence, whether in dazzling brilliancy or in quiet serenity, now wishes to appear to all creation through us. We move forth into a new flow of life that is Christ-centered, where we put the Christ precepts into practice, respond to our neighbor in compassionate Christ love, and dissipate the darkness through sharing the Christ-light.

It is essential, I think, in all forms of prayer, contemplation, or meditation to release all controls to God. Even the methods and techniques are God's to give to us, and we should be forever willing to abandon or modify any form. A veritable network of devices has been created by humans in their long search to ensnare the Infinite, and there is nothing sacred about this reticulation. What is sacred is the point of contact with God. Since God wants

The Meditation Experience

this contact much more than we do, we only need to be willing to trust God to open up the way.

There is much I have not covered concerning the meditation experience. I have not talked about the seven nerve centers (*chakras*) and the corresponding colors of these centers. Nor have I discussed the forces within our cerebrospinal system known as the *kundalini shakti,* a mysterious fire of love that rises up within us through daily, sincere periods of meditation and which transports us into a new land of expanded consciousness. This is basically a beginner's manual, and those concepts, coming from the Eastern mystics, belong farther along the pathway of the inner journey. They are explained in numerous books on meditation for any who are interested, and there is no reason for the Christian to be afraid of any of these.

I sincerely hope that what I have offered to the one who has stayed with me this far is a realization that the dark night of separation can be over, that God's presence is available to us in such a way as to unify all our faculties, bring us peace and joy, and help us accomplish in this world as holy sons or daughters of God the tasks we came here to do. A great portion of the psyche of many persons is starved. Such people are in constant pain and turmoil and often question the worth of life. No amount of reasoning can change their condition. As Marshall McLuhan reminds us, we are subjected to the tyranny of mass media and find ourselvs more and more hopelessly enmeshed in our own extended nervous systems. There is a way out. Liberation and peace can be ours. This book is an effort to show that nourishment is available for the part of us which cries with eternal hunger.

In the final analysis neither prayer nor meditation can be acquired or taught. Each person has his or her own pathway to follow and must learn to be true to that path. The essence of the inner life is surrender to the Christ-Spirit. The Spirit will lead each of us, gently and carefully, on the way that is best for us. Carried on those

Journey to Inner Space

tender wings of love, we can rest assured that no lasting harm will ever befall us on our journey and that someday we will arrive home. Waiting there are the welcoming arms of the Father God, who stirred our hearts into their restless seeking and who has fueled our longings through the long night of our quest. And there is sounded forth the joyous proclamation, "Son [daughter], you are always with me, and all that is mine is yours." Enter now into the joy of your inheritance.

Chapter 10
The Ladder of Prayer

Prayer is the language of the soul. Everyone prays, even the atheist, for we can no more refrain from praying than we can refrain from breathing without seriously altering life as we know it. Prayer always takes the form best suited to the need and temperament of the individual, but it should be recognized that until prayer becomes a growth in consciousness and extended awareness, away from self and things and toward God, it will not succeed.

Many people look for a way out of their troubles and discords. Sometimes they try prayer as a short route to overcoming problems. However, there is never an easy way out of a serious problem, and indeed there should not be. The problems in our lives, regardless of what caused them, have the capacity to purify our spirits and raise our love to a state of authentic purity. Their instant removal might be much worse for us. We need our problems and conflicts to help us grow and evolve into more perfected states. Prayer does overcome problems, but never in a magical way apart from us. Through prayer we find the strength to meet a problem and use it for good, rather than allowing the problem to use and defeat us.

Many people hope prayer will provide them with an insular protection against dangers, diseases, and defeats. But prayer will not work in this fashion. Remember, prayer did not save Jesus from the cross. Prayer does not make us totally immune to the negative forces that stalk the world but it does make us spiritually conscious of our true identity and the source of our real strength. The spiritual life in its early stages is a walk ever-alternating between the valleys of the shadow and the lighted mountain peaks, even for the devotee of prayer, although the day will come when we will dwell forever on the peaks if we persist in a prayer that is directed beyond our immediate wants.

What then is the purpose of prayer if it will not get us what we want? There is no single purpose of prayer, because prayer is always changing in form and growing with our learning. At its highest, prayer fuses into total communication and oneness with God and becomes formless. At its lowest, prayer is merely question or entreaty.

Let us explore the ladder of prayer and attempt to understand it as a path toward God and his world in which the self becomes truly fulfilled by a recognition of the Christ within. Do not despair nor deplore if you find yourself now standing on any of the lower rungs. Everyone stands there at one time or another. Give thanks for all that has been as well as all that is now, for thus you prepare yourself for the longest stride of the soul—its exploration into God.

In the discipline of the inner journey, certain patterns of prayer seem to emerge in order, as demonstrated by this ladder:

| CHRIST ME |
| ABIDE ME |
| USE ME |
| FORGIVE ME |
| GIVE ME |
| SAVE ME |
| HELP ME |

The Ladder of Prayer

Some of the rungs imbricate, but as you mount the ladder you become aware that you are moving out of the morass of the selfish, desperate me to the me that has achieved a sense of personal realization and freedom. From this emerges the me who is dedicated to service to others, until at length the me is lifted above its world of desires, things, and goals into its ultimate holiness and purity as a son or daughter of God, fully at home and one with the Father. At this point the me is transcended, the I becomes a thou, and the ladder ends, for our learning is completed. Let us now begin our climb.

Note: [An explanation of the use of masculine terms is in order. The Judaic-Christian culture from which these terms emerged was patriarchical. Only the male had landed rights and legatee privileges. The female was chattel. I abhor such nonegalitarianism and fully believe in the equality of the sexes. But in higher spiritual goals all sexual distinctions are merged and transcended with everyone receiving a full inheritance in the Kingdom. Working from a historical reference it makes no sense to say *sons and daughters,* but gnomically this is accurate, for everyone is included in God's great plan, male and female alike. Where I have deviated from inclusive language into masculine forms (as in denoting God as Father) I have done so because these forms communicate a historical significance that cannot be ignored, and likewise they communicate a spiritual significance to me personally that I cannot dismiss.]

Help Me. The old wartime adage "There are no atheists in foxholes" is a reminder to us that we all have times and situations in life so desperate and terrifying that we are literally propelled into praying. Sometimes this prayer takes the form of talking to God, whether there is any previous reference point or acquaintance with God. Occasionally it may take the form of talking to someone else who is a person of faith, even asking him or her to pray for us, because we have such small faith in our own prayers.

Journey to Inner Space

Though I place this prayer at the lowest rung of the ladder, I do not mean it is the lowest form of prayer. Rather it is the prayer most native to all of us. We all have times when we need help and deliverance, and who is God if not a God of deliverance? God does not despise our prayers for help, nor does he condemn us because we wait to turn to him when we are in trouble. Even after we have mounted higher on the ladder, we may find ourselves returning to this prayer or asking others to pray for us because we are momentarily too weak or uncertain to pray for ourselves. As long as we are in these bodies, we will continue to face circumstances that will challenge us beyond our mortal strength. As we grow in our prayer life, instead of imploring or beseeching from the abyss of a barren land, we will know that God is always more ready to help his children than his children are ready to receive his help. Thus, in time our prayers for help will rise from the confidence of a child of God, rather than from an alien who feels cut off in a far country.

Often our requests for help need purification. A man talked to me once because he had prayed to God for relief from his financial dilemma and concluded, when help was not immediately forthcoming, that God did not want to help him. His tangled, snarled problems had been years in the making, however, and were the result of a poverty consciousness on his part. He needed a redirecting of consciousness at the level of material wealth; otherwise to rescue him from one dilemma would only be freeing him to flounder into another. God can help us financially, but not until we climb far enough up the ladder of prayer to say, "Use me. Take these gifts you have given me, which I have mismanaged, and use them in your way and for your glory. I am taking my hands off and giving you complete control." If we seal this prayer with a pledge to make a regular contribution to some phase of God's work, in time God will work a new consciousness and a new spirit in us that will set us free as wise and willing stewards of our material riches.

The Ladder of Prayer

Before we leave this rung of the ladder, let us be sure we understand that we *always* have the help of God. By claiming the abiding presence of God through prayer and meditation, we are also claiming all that we need or want.

Save Me. This is essentially the same as the prayer "help me," but it achieves a higher dimension, and it also incorporates some basic dangers which must be avoided. The Old Testament is replete with prayers to be saved. These range in meaning from the most ordinary, everyday or secular sense to historical salvation for Israel. Out of such prayers grew the expectation of a Savior who would come to deliver his people. In the New Testament, salvation is understood as accomplished by an act of God in human history, namely, the life, death, and resurrection of Jesus Christ.

In post-Reformation Christianity a salvation cult developed expressing the illusion of the elect, that God's grace is available only for those who find and hold the right set of beliefs. Traces of such fatuous superiority continue to live on in modern-day conservative Christianity, dividing humanity in two categories, the saved and the unsaved, and making salvation the leitmotiv and cynosure of religion. The saved are, of course, those who will go to heaven, and the unsaved are those who will go to hell.

Any prayer posited on such misanthropic predilections is both narcissistic and untenable. It fails to recognize the universality of God who inhabits all creation and whose grace is free to all persons beyond any religious beliefs or convictions. No person can ever hope for salvation unless he can first of all recognize that there is only one God in this world and that God is the divine parent of all humanity, not just a select few. It is pure nonsense to imagine that only Christians will be saved, only Jews, only Buddhists, only Baptists, or only anything, when in very fact the Spirit of God inhabits every soul and is making provision for every soul ultimately to come home.

I had an experience once while traveling in the Islamic

countries of southwest Asia which helped me to see that God's plan is greater than any I had envisioned. As I visited the mosques and saw hundreds of faithful Muslims praying with noisy and sincere devotion to Allah with a religious fervor not always equaled by Christians, I knew they were praying to the same God that I always addressed. Would making them Christians increase their religious zeal, improve their status in life, give them greater peace? Perhaps. But were they lost and damned because they did not have Christ?

"Lord God," I prayed, "what about these people?"

As clearly as though he stood at my side the answer was spoken into my consciousness with such unmistakable clarity that I have remembered it vividly. "If you had been born in this country, you would in all likelihood be Muslim. Do not think by accident of your birth or culture you are any better or more favored than they. I love all my children, I hear all their prayers, and I have a holy, indestructible plan for everyone."

There is no virtue in a prayer or an activity that seeks salvation of the self and stops there. We all need to be saved from our sins, but not so we can feel superior to others or force our way on others. The whole point of salvation is to serve God. Just as Jesus came not to be served but to serve and give his life as a ransom for many, so we must do the same when we elect to follow him, dispensing with all notions that there is any select body called the saved or any unfortunate body called the lost. When we truly pray, we make entry into the minds and hearts of *all* God's children, and any prayer that draws lines of exclusivism or holds us apart from another is prayer misused. The only legitimate use of the prayer "save me" comes when we are willing to add, "that I might serve you better and love as you do." When we can say that, we are ready to mount to the next rung on the ladder of prayer.

Give Me. Prayers that seek favors of God are essentially futile. When we pray to God to bring us peace on earth, to heal the sick, to give us rain (or to stop the rain), to destroy our enemies, or to give us any material thing, we are predicating our prayers on a false concept of God which says that he sits on a throne as some capricious despot who must be curried into granting favors. God is not withholding anything from us, and God has nothing more to give us than he is presently giving.

Let us begin then to correct the concept that we need to tell or ask the all-knowing God for what we need. If we need health, we must recognize that God is all-health. If we need bread, we must recognize that God is the living bread. If we want friends, we must recognize that God is the provider of companionship. Therefore, if we have God we have all that we need or want. The only legitimate prayer of asking is for more of God. By turning within daily for acknowledgment and awareness of God, we are receiving all the effects of God's presence. Our desire for specific gifts must always be surrendered in our greater desire for God, for nothing less than God can truly satisfy. Our lives are incomplete if we seek the gifts apart from the Giver.

When we pray for things, no matter how worthy these things may be, we are actually praying for idols and hoping by them to reach God. Our only request in prayer should be to ask to receive what God has already given and to accept what is already here. True prayer is forgetting those things which we think we need, or to let these go into God's hands, so that we will have no other gods before him. True prayer is letting go of our requests, stepping aside, and offering up to God the totality of our being. That surrendered being becomes the altar of God where all our wants disappear in the discovery that we have everything.

Forgive Me. Through much futile effort it finally becomes apparent that all our praying for help or salvation has been largely ineffective because it has lacked the one requirement of true prayer—confession. We can never receive from God the gifts that God longs to give us until we are willing to have removed from our lives whatever blocks the flow of God's love. We do this by turning to the prayer that is the key to all our future praying, "Forgive me." This prayer of confession rises out of the realization of our total helplessness to be all that we want to be, all that we truly are. We have discovered our inability to forgive, because we are too deeply entrenched in self-recrimination and its partner, judgment (which is but a result of self-recrimination, since what we cannot forgive in ourselves we project into the world as judgments against those who remind us of our own worst side). We are indeed in a hopeless state unless we realize the possibility of forgiveness. Forgiveness then becomes our rescuer.

As we realize the impossibility of being able to forgive as fully and completely as we ought and turn to God for help, God not only forgives us, he awakens in us the ability to forgive others. More accurately, he helps us see that in order to experience his forgiveness for ourselves we must offer our lives as channels for his forgiving love to flow through and into the lives of others.

The prayer for forgiveness follows two avenues. We *give over* to God anything in ourselves and others toward which we are less than wholly loving. The result is that God grants us the power to *look over* what earlier we called evil. We do not have the perception to know as God knows, not even when it comes to ourselves. When we pray for forgiveness, we *give over* to God in order to *look over* what our human ego has falsely taught us to believe.

The teachings of Jesus on forgiveness are explicit. He leaves no illusions that permit us to harbor grudges, resentments, or hostilities, no matter how justified they seem. His demonstration of forgiveness was a powerful witness of his teaching, when from the cross he prayed God's forgiveness for those who had placed him there. He was acknowledging that forgiveness is a work of God, a sacred activity beyond the human capacity to perform alone.

Yet forgiveness is not just something that God does to us

and through us. God is forgiveness itself. This means that only God has the power to transmute human error and sin into forgiveness, for only God can enter into our human condition with the power to redeem. Only God's love in us can help us love the unlovely, the unloveable, and the unloved. Our work is then to do no work, but to *let go and let come* into our lives that loving forgiveness, which is none other than God himself.

In Arthur Miller's play *After the Fall* we meet a woman named Holga. She has gone through the bombings of war and the horrors of a concentration camp, but she still faces life with faith and hope. When asked how she can do this, she recalls a dream that haunted her recurrently near the end of the war. In her dream an idiot child followed her about, clutching at her clothes, trying to climb upon her lap. Holga recognized that the child represented her life and knew that somehow she had to take it on her lap and kiss its horrible, broken face. When she did, she was free of the nightmare and ready to live. She says, "I think one must finally take one's life in one's arms."

"Forgive me" is the prayer that helps us take our own life, and the lives of others, in our arms and bestow upon all the kiss of God's healing love.

Use Me. The first four rungs on the ladder of prayer deal with forms that center on the pray-er. Now we are ready to move from a self-centered preoccupation with our own needs and wants to an expanded concern for others. The prayer "use me" takes us into the servant role of caring for others and into the priestly role of praying for others.

Yet even intercessory prayer is partially prayer for one's own self, for what we do as an intercessor is to free our brother and sister from our own projected guilts and angers. On the lower rungs of the ladder we may have been judging our brothers and sisters, sometimes blaming them for our problems, sometimes envying them for getting ahead of us, and sometimes hating them for being in our way. Now we are face-to-face with the realization that we can go no farther on the ladder of prayer until we let ourselves be used as channels of forgiveness and healing for any burden or blame we have placed on another. Thus, the prayer "use me" is an extension of the previous prayer "forgive me." Through this prayer we place ourselves under the sovereign rule of God to be used as his channels of forgiveness, service, and prayer for the world.

An effective way to pray for another is by using the Golden Rule: I offer this one all that I would wish to receive if I were in his/her place. We seek to enter into the other person's life with total empathy and compassion. We hold out our hands to everyone we have disliked and from whom we have been separated. We bless them, and we accept a blessing from them. We refuse to see anyone as enemies or alien, for we know that this view costs us the most priceless possession in the universe, God. In prayer we release everyone as enemies, past or present, and claim them as brothers and sisters.

What about explicit requests for others? It is no different for them than it is for us. The only thing anyone needs is more of God and a fuller realization of God's kingdom. Therefore, let us not agonize over specific demands or supplications, no matter how worthy these may seem. We wear ourselves out praying in such a manner.

Albert E. Day says that when we pray for others we are offering God our consciousness as his way to their consciousness. It is difficult to stand by and watch people suffer from pain, be blighted by ignorance, waste their lives in useless activities, and drag families and friends down with them into a mire of sorrow and degradation. But God never trespasses another person's freedom and neither should we. In spite of best intentions and well-meant support, we cannot really help another until that person is ready to help himself or herself. The best we can do is to offer our finite consciousness to God in confidence that God will use our human channel in some way to activate his life within others.

As we stand on the rung of the ladder and pray, "Use

me," we are giving God the opportunity to bring through our own yielded will and consciousness something more glorious and far-reaching than we ourselves could ever plan. It is also at this level of prayer we receive our "marching orders." When our yielding is complete and pure, God will begin to reveal to us other specific tasks or assignments that he wants us to do. This comes as we enter into the spirit of the highest spoken prayer ever to be offered, "Father, not my will, but thine, be done." In final analysis this is the only prayer that we can ever use and know that it is absolutely right for every time, every person, and every situation. It is a prayer that pours out self and offers to God an empty vessel for his filling. It is this prayer, when sincerely prayed, that carries us to the top of the ladder, for not until we know what it is to put God's will ahead of our own and ultimately let God's will become ours, can we go into the higher realms of prayer and receive the holiness that is ours.

Abide Me. When Jesus finished his great prayer of surrender in the Garden of Gethsemane, he was able to go forth to his trial and crucifixion with serenity and courage. His Christhood had fully taken over, and he lived thenceforth in full consciousness of the abiding presence. His one moment of regressive despair from the cross when he cried, "My God, why has thou forsaken me?" was quickly transmuted by his surrendering prayer, "Father, into thy hands I commit my spirit." He was sustained by the abiding presence, which never left him.

By the ladder of prayer we rise slowly to a place of true humility where we lay aside all judgments, all little gods, all resentments, and all desires except the one desire for God. No longer do we come to God with the request for him to be our servant and do our bidding. No longer do we say, "God, I know what I need, and you do not, so I will tell you." We know from experience that this kind of praying does not work, that it is stupidity on our part to approach the infinite intelligence that created this universe in that manner. Now we come to God in prayer simply to realize more and more of God's presence, for we realize we want and need this more than anything else. We have learned that true prayer is more than asking, more than seeking, more than wanting. True prayer is realizing that God is revealing, unfolding, and disclosing himself to us, that he is abiding us forever.

The word *abide* means "to continue in one place with expectancy." When we affirm that God abides us, we are saying that God inhabits us, indwells us, tabernacles us, continues in us forever and always. Once we have the consciousness of his abiding presence, we live in a glorious hope and expectancy that sees life becoming more wonderful with each passing day. It is only a step now to the greatest and the final learning, the place of our total oneness with God.

As I look back over my years there runs through me a feeling of wonder and gratitude that some abiding presence sustained and protected me always, even when in my consciousness I stood at the lower rungs of the ladder. But the discovery that I do indeed "dwell in the shelter of the most high and abide in the shadow of the Almighty" was a discovery of journeying to my inner space. As I gradually lost the sense of Rodney's being separate and apart from God, I could hear God say, "All that I have is yours. We are one. You are in me, and I am in you." I am convinced that this is God's word to each of us, if we will come to that inner sanctuary where we can hear him speak.

Christ Me. Jesus not only knew the Christ in himself, he saw the Christ in everyone else. Jesus became what each of us is destined to be, a Christ, and he remains with us in Spirit to show us the way to God and to the Christ of our inner being. The Christ has taken many forms and has been known by different names, but that need not concern us. We know the Christ as Jesus who came to this earth two thousand years ago with the triumphant message of God's love, uniting us to the reality of our true identity. At

The Ladder of Prayer

that place of knowing, all illusions end, and we come to apprehend our intended glory and to accept our true divinity as a holy son or daughter of God. We stand now on the highest rung of the ladder of prayer.

This final rung is the place where we are fully Christ-like, where we recognize the Christ in ourselves and in all others. At first we are unable to live continuously and consistently at this height. It is a fragmentary, sidereal kind of experience, so tentative and fleeting at its inception as to seem almost illusionary. But as we learn to drop our solipsistic concerns and pursue the silence of our inner being beyond all customary bounds, there gradually emerges from the undergrowth of our landscapes and the corridors of our dreams a love so pervasive and powerful that it drenches our souls with a quietude and a hallowed respect for all things. All former diffidence and uncertainty begin to fade, and we are slowly filled with a transcending joy and ecstatic delight. We see creation through the eyes of God, and simultaneously with that vision we begin to merge into oneness with all things until there is no distinction between I and Thou. All parts become perfectly blended into the whole, the transistory becomes permanent, and time is fused into eternity. We know ourselves now to be a part of everything in the created order—every human being, every animal, every flower, every rock, every grain of sand, every star in the universe. We also know ourselves to be a part of the Creator, for at the highest rung of the ladder God declares to us, "You are my beloved son, my beloved daughter, in whom I am well pleased."

You may wonder as we mounted the ladder of prayer what became of thanksgiving. Do you not see now that it was present at each and every step? Did not your heart fill with appreciation as God delivered you from your prison and taught you to use your freedom wisely? Did you not experience a surge of thanksgiving as you found yourself forgiven and made a partner with him in a ministry of love to the world? Did not your soul overflow in gratitude as you sensed his abiding and discovered your own identity? Thanksgiving is the current that underlies and permeates all God-directed prayer, and "Thank you, Father," becomes the litany of every step we take. When we have journeyed enough times to the still point within and sense this as our true home, our lives melt into a crucible of gratitude, with every resistance melted in the face of the incredible reception of love that encompasses us at the altar of our inner space.

Now we have reached the top of the ladder, oddly enough not by climbing at all but by journeying within ourselves. Our learning is now completed, heaven is before us. We have recognized who we are and what we have. We have come to our own Christhood. The long, lonely journey is over. We are home at last.

Chapter 11
A Night in the Hills
(a meditation on the Lord's Prayer and Psalm 23)

Two of the greatest documents in the Christian faith are the Lord's Prayer and the Twenty-third Psalm. Portions or all of each can be quoted by nearly every person, whether religious, agnostic, or atheistic. Each holds a unique place in literature for its quality of beauty and depth of religious content, and each is the common ground that all Christians share with reverence, no matter what differences may separate.

Psalm 23 was written many years before Jesus lived, and it became a much loved hymn of the Hebrew people. This is not surprising, for one has the feeling in reading this psalm today that it is expressing a truth so profound and timeless that it momentarily lifts the veil that mysteriously separates the finite from the infinite and lets us see into the very heart of God. The psalm is a great lesson on prayer, for it is prayer itself, a prayer that God may have uttered within the consciousness of an unknown pray-er, perhaps an Israelite shepherd during the lonely night watches of guarding his sheep.

In this psalm there is no appeal to God for anything, no asking, no demanding, no begging. There is rather the recognition that God is, and because God is, we have everything we need or want. Limitations, troubles, needs, and fears are not denied, but the psalmist asserts we can pass through all these things safely. Why? Because God is with us. Throughout the psalm we never reach for God or beg God to do anything. We simply make confident assertion that we have God and his continuing, never-failing love forever. This is the truth God gave to the psalmist to be shared with the world.

The highest prayer is not what we say but rather what God says within us. When God is able to pray through us instead of our trying to pray through God, then prayer becomes what it is meant to be—the voice of the Infinite speaking through the finite channels of our own awareness. This must surely have been the means by which the Twenty-third Psalm came to the shepherd, as well as the means by which the Lord's Prayer came to Jesus. God spoke through the listening soul of each, for their solitary experiences in the wilderness had trained them in the mystical consciousness that is capable of hearing God.

Jesus grew up thoroughly familiar with the Scriptures (the Old Testament). As a young Jewish lad, he was conscientiously trained and educated in the synagogue, so we know that he knew the Twenty-third Psalm. Although he never quoted it directly, he used much of its imagery in his teachings, even applying the metaphor of the shepherd to himself.

It has occurred to me that possibly Jesus constructed his great prayer from the Twenty-third Psalm, for they closely parallel each other in form and content. Perhaps during one of his nocturnal retreats, when he drew apart from the disciples to pray and meditate, he began to sense God speaking to him through the timeworn and much-loved lines of this old psalm.

Later, when the disciples asked Jesus to teach them to pray, it was a natural thing for him to share with them the carefully formed prayer that God had given to him, offering it to them, not merely for recitation, but as a scaffolding upon which their future praying could be built. After all, Jesus was a carpenter with a carpenter's appreciation for strong foundations, frameworks, and

A Night in the Hills

scaffolds. The Lord's Prayer was presented as a foundation for the kind of prayer that would make the disciples conscious of the presence of God and ultimately elevate them to the level of spiritual communication which is beyond human words and thoughts.

But let us allow Jesus to share the story with us, a story which we will not find in the written records that exist today, but, which through our meditative imagination, he might unfold to us as follows:

I waited until the others had fallen asleep and the fire had burned down to a few lambent embers before I arose. Moving noiselessly through the mounds of sleeping men who were huddled under their robes with feet toward the moribund embers, I made my way to the edge of the lake and waited for a moment beside the inky expanse of water, listening to the waves suck thirstily at the shore. I was both restless and quiescent. Something in the solitude of the sea and quiet of the terrestrial undulations was luring me away from that consociate family at the fire that had been with me faithfully now for several months. We had grown close in spite of our amalgamation and differences, but there was an area of experiential reference that was largely untouched in our fraternal sharings, and that area was prayer. Some of the men are almost agoraphobic, terrified of solitude and silence, and when I begin to talk of speaking and listening to God, they mark my words with uneasy deference and make haste to change the trend of the conversation as quickly as they can. If I could teach them to seek God within their own being, they could share this experience with others. Nothing I might say to them is of greater consequence to our future efforts than the necessity of prayer at a deep level, but all my words sound stiffly inadequate and scabrous when I try to open the subject. "O Yahweh, God of our fathers, how may I teach them to pray?"

I began to ascend the gentle slope of the hill, moving through a copse of cypress trees that nestled in a swale like black, feathered panaches. After several minutes of easy climbing, I paused in an open spot to listen again to the night sounds. A little creature was stirring in the grass beside my path. A wave of cool air wafted up from the lake and fanned my cheek like a caress from God's own hand. The velvet sky, punctured with stars, was beginning to brighten against the hills, and I knew that shortly the moon would rise to invade that sidereal canopy that arched above the world like an ebony bejeweled robe. I found an outcropping of rocks where I sat down and looked back in the direction of the lake to the flickering pinpoint of fire where my little flock slept. My flock! How I loved that little band of twelve men, and how I longed to open the door for them to the greater expanses of their own soul.

I began to chant softly the psalm "The Lord is my shepherd, I shall not want." Sometimes the disciples would sing the psalm with me as we hiked through the open fields or sat around the evening fire, their faces gentle with unfeigned appreciation for its literate beauty and the nascence of mystical piety shining in their eyes.

Suddenly it struck me with the stunning force of a divine riposte flung into the hiatus of my earlier prayer that they needed a model prayer, an archetype for the widening prayer which ultimately needs no words, but which cannot begin without them. They needed words of such quality and standard that they would have a foundation on which to build all their future praying, a prayer to which they could return over and over again, just as my carpenter father always returned to the basic and simple mathematic formulas, even though he was building an edifice of spectacular dimensions.

I raised my eyes to the crown of stars and cried, "O God, teach me your perfect prayer for me, for my disciples, for all humanity." As I waited, the acuity of my surroundings began to fade, and I was conscious of a warmth spreading upward from my spine and along my shoulders, which always signified that God was going to speak to me from that particular level of my consciousness that I have

A Night in the Hills

learned to identify clearly and unmistakably as the infinite voice.

Jesus, you are my son. So are they. I am the Heavenly Father of all. Teach them to call me Father. I am not a God so removed and separate that they dare not utter my name. I am Abba, daddy. I belong to all, for I am in all. Teach them to look for me within themselves and in one another, in the heaven that dwells in the heart of every person.

I trembled as the words flowed from my lips, "Our Father who art in heaven."

Yes, that is right. I am the Father in the heaven of your being, of all being. The centuries are dark with the futile search that has been conducted for me in the outer realm. Let everyone realize that I am within every soul. Teach them to bless their inner lives and the inner lives of one another with a hallowed consciousness of my presence, so that there shall be no sense of separation from me or from one another in my sons and daughters. They have forgotten who they are. When they pray, it must be a reminder to them of who I am, who they are, and what I would have my children do. I want them to return to me and let me hallow my name in their lives. The kingdom of heaven is within, and that is where I am.

"Hallowed be thy name," I cried out. "O Father God you cause us to lie down in green pastures. You lead us beside the still waters." How easily the old familiar words came crowding back.

My kingdom is the green pasture of your souls. It is that place where your every need is met, your every want supplied, where you feed and want no more. My will is the still water of your being. The highest peace you can ever know is in the knowing and the doing of my will.

"Thy Kingdom come, thy will be done on earth, as it is in heaven," I prayed. "Of course, before the kingdom can come into the outer realm, it must come into the inner being. Your will must be done in the heaven of our human souls, before it can be expressed in the world around us. O Father, you prepare a table before me in the presence of my enemies. You anoint my head with oil. My cup overflows." In my eagerness, I had jumped ahead into the lines of gratitude and adoration from the psalm, the place where the guest extends grateful thanks to the host for all that has been provided for his comfort.

I am always nourishing my children, not only in their spirits but in their minds and bodies as well. They do not need to beg me for material benefits. Have I not endowed this earth with an abundant supply? There is more than enough for all, if it is cared for responsibly. The earth is created to replenish itself, to feed my little ones. Teach them to be simpler in their wants, less expansive in their demands. They do not need to beseech me with long lists and requests. I give without their asking. When they seek my kingdom first, all needs are supplied.

"Give us this day our daily bread. Is that enough?"

Yes, that is enough. The daily bread, not the bread from yesterday nor the bread for tomorrow, but the daily bread. Fear of yesterday, anxiety for tomorrow—these are your enemies. In the midst of these enemies, I spread a table with the daily bread and the assurance that there is bread enough and to spare in my house.

"Father God," I answered, "you are always restoring our souls and ever leading us in the paths of righteousness for your name's sake. How can I teach them to follow you in these paths? What is the way?"

The way is forgiveness. Forgiveness is the key. Not a forgiveness born from one's feelings of superiority or condescending pity for another, but a forgiveness born out of my own forgiving love. Humans cannot forgive on their own. They are too deeply entrenched in self-condemnation and judgments, the latter being the projection of the former. They must allow me to forgive them, and then offer their lives to me as channels by which my forgiving love can be carried to others.

"Forgive us for the way we have mistreated ourselves and others, as we forgive those who have mistreated us. Is that it?"

A Night in the Hills

Precisely. All persons are in debt. No one can alleviate his own burden of debt. There is a long trail of efforts to repay where some in the past have tried to assume the burden of indebtedness on their own shoulders. It is too much for them. No matter how they try, in their human strength they cannot atone for all their past mistakes and trespasses. Therefore, they must trust me to do it for them. I will teach them to be as forgiving to others as they would have me be to them, as indeed I already am.

"Father, it is clear to me now. You are the God of deliverance. You want us to come home to you. More than that, you are helping us come home to you. Even though I walk through the valley of the shadow of death, I will fear no evil, for you are with me; your rod and staff comfort me."

I will never tempt my children, Jesus. I only seek to deliver them from their mistakes and illusions. I want to free them. I want to loosen every chain that binds, every thought that cripples, every fear that restricts. I want to deliver them from every evil, the evil of their own sense of separation from me and the evil of their tyranny over one another, the evil of the thing they call death, which is only a door into a larger consciousness of me. Teach them this, my son.

"Lead us not into temptation, but deliver us from evil. It is so easy after all. Just a simple knowing what you stand ready to do for your children. O Father God, my heart overflows!"

My Son, I love you.

The moon had risen now into the dome of the heavens, leaving a silver wake across the Galilean sea. My altar of shadowy rocks had emerged into the translucent glow and stood starkly revealed. I sat motionless for a long while and watched the moon dip lower into the sea and begin to disappear.

"Surely goodness and mercy shall follow me all the days of my life, and I will dwell in the house of the Lord forever." The prayer had never been more profoundly uttered by me than it was at that moment. Now I knew that the kingdom is forever, God's power is forever, God's glory is forever. And that kingdom, power, and glory are in every human soul, forever, blessing each life with an abundance of goodness and mercy and guiding our wandering, erratic steps back to the Father's house. I sat transfixed, no longer aware of time or space, lifted from all consciousness of place or circumstance into a timelessness where an incredible love invaded and filled me with a sense of utter peace.

The eastern sky was pinkish gray with the early flushes of dawn when I finally stood up and moved down the hillside. Someone had nourished the latent sparks of the fire into a roaring blaze. Some of the men were up, others were emerging from beneath their robes, eyes puffy with sleep. Andrew, who was fueling the fire, saw me approaching and came striding to meet me. Peering into my face, he cried reproachfully, "Master, you did not sleep!"

I laid my hand gently on his tousled hair, thinking how much I loved this steady, hardworking man. "It was better than sleep," I assured him.

Simon and Judas, my wild Zealots, came running up from the lake, where they had been swimming. Drops of water shone in their long hair and beards and ran in glistening streams over their muscular nakedness as they toweled off with their burnouses.

Then Judas saw me. Tucking his robe carelessly around his slim waist, he strode across the circle to where I stood with Andrew, his handsome dark eyes flashing that warmth of affection for me that he gave to no one else. Dear fiery, fierce, protective Judas, always wanting my attention, always attempting to be the cynosure of the group, always trying to control. I loved him, but he caused me greater anxiety and apprehension than all the others.

"I woke in the night, and you were gone," he said half-accusingly. "You have not slept. Where have you been?"

A Night in the Hills

"Come to the fire, Judas," I invited. "Help me prepare breakfast. Later I will tell you."

He liked working with me. Strutting at my side with self-importance, he called out loudly to the rest, "Jesus and I will do breakfast today."

When the meal was finished, we sat in a circle as we generally did so that I might outline plans and schedule for the day. We were several days' journey from Jerusalem, so there was not the restive urgency in the group which usually sprang up when we neared a city or village. Instead, a kind of rural torpor had settled over them. Peter yawned and stretched huge arms. Blinking into the sun that was now climbing above the hills, he scratched contentedly and commented, "Nice day, huh?"

"The Master is going to share something," announced Judas presumptuously. "He has been leaving us at night and going away by himself."

Twelve pairs of eyes fastened on me, some curious, some half-embarassed at Judas' impetuous need to uncover everything I did. Somewhat surprised, I looked at him and asked, "What do you wish to know, Judas?"

"Where you go. What you do." He looked around the circle defensively. "We are his disciples. We should be sharing everything with him. We have a right to know. He needs our protection, if nothing else."

"I go into the hills to be alone, Judas." I looked at the others and smiled gently. "There are certain times we should each be alone. In the solitude we discover God."

A few lowered their eyes self-consciously. Not Judas. His look had softened, but the black eyes still challenged. "Do you pray all night, Master?" His tone was both curious and caustic.

"Yes, but not the talking kind of prayer. I spend much time in the silence, listening to God, listening to God's world, waiting to hear that inner voice within me, which is God."

"Do—do you always hear God?" Philip asked hesitantly.

"Always. Not always in the same way. But always God

speaks. I could not know what to do if God did not tell me. Where do you think I receive my teaching, my direction, my sense of purpose, my knowing who I am? Even the naming of you as disciples was given to me by God." Looking at Judas, I added, "All of you."

Everyone was silent now. A dove whistled in startled flight over our heads, in her soaring dropping a gray feather which settled slowly into the center of our circle. They watched it drift lazily to the ground without comprehension of it. Plainly they were thinking of what I had just said.

Then John raised his eyes, brown pools of morning light. His beautiful young face was eager. There was no muddled saintliness in this one, as in some of the others. Here was the clear purity of a true mystic, a quiet, unassuming goodness that had impressed me from the moment I first saw him mending fishing nets by the lake with James and his father Zebedee. "Master," he spoke quietly yet distinctly. "Will you teach us to pray?"

A collective affinity seemed to rise from the twelve for a moment and reached out toward me. The faces that looked into mine were trusting, the eyes fueled with hidden longings. Even Judas looked wistful.

The moment had come, the high moment for which I had yearned. My heart was full. "Yes, dear friends," I began, "I will teach you to pray. I will teach you what God has taught me.

"When you pray, do not be like the hypocrites, for they love to stand and pray in the synagogues and at the street corners, that they may be seen by others. Since they are seeking the attention of others, they have their reward. But when you pray, enter into the solitude of the hills or the woods, where, away from all outer distractions, you can pray to your Heavenly Father in the secret of your own being. God, who sees into the secret place, will give you what you are seeking. Do not heap up empty, monotonous phrases in your praying, and do not go to the Father with your long list of requests. He knows what you need before

A Night in the Hills

you ask him. Although prayer is much more than words, this is the place to begin. Therefore, pray like this:

> *"Our Father, who art in heaven,*
> *Hallowed be thy name.*
> *Thy Kingdom come,*
> *Thy will be done,*
> > *on earth as it is in heaven.*
> *Give us this day our daily bread;*
> *and forgive us our debts,*
> > *As we also have forgiven our debtors;*
> *And lead us not into temptation,*
> *But deliver us from evil."*

When I finished, there was a long, unbroken silence. Thomas spoke first. "Master, we must learn that prayer, so we can say it correctly, with the right words and all."

"We will learn it," I assured him, "but it is not repeating the words that matters. It is understanding that these words are the beginning of an adventure that will free your spirits to soar into the limitless expanse of the great God who created this universe, where you will be beyond the limit of words. This is the place from which you begin, as well as the place to which you return to check your progress from time to time."

I looked around the circle, silently blessing each face that was uplifted to me with the same eager trust I had often seen in the faces of little children when they gathered to listen to my stories. I knew that the seed had been planted. It would grow in time. Each man would learn in good time to pray from the depth of his own soul, for the time would surely come for each of us when prayer would be our only anchor, the only reality left.

"We will spend this day in quietness," I suggested. "Let each of you seek a solitary spot where you can meditate, pray, and contemplate. This will be a day apart from everyone else, a day alone with God. This evening we will come together and share what the day has meant."

Journey to Inner Space

I sensed their silent agreement to my proposal. Quietly they rose and moved off singly toward the lake, through the woods, or into the hills. Judas was the last to leave, making a pretense of being busy at the fire. I knew he wanted to speak to me. His cohort and constant ally Simon had already disappeared. "What is it, Judas?" I asked. "Are you staying in camp?"

"Could—could I be with you?" He kicked his sandal into the dust, clearly embarrassed at making his request, hating the weakness in himself that prompted it. But I understood. This one who lived so energetically in the exterior world was terrified of solitude. He had blocked the avenues to his interiority so long, he dared not begin to explore them. I wondered if he ever could.

I put my arm around his strong shoulders. "Yes, Judas. How kind of you to realize that I need a companion today." Together we walked toward the hills.

Chapter 12
Water from Deep Wells

(Note: I have made it a practice to meditate before I write, because I have discovered this releases the creative flow and puts me in touch with higher thoughts and greater ideas. The following materials were given to me in my meditation periods during the time I was working on this book with the instruction to include them in the manuscript itself.

Variations of this experience of "receiving" are available to anyone, I believe, who meditates or prays by listening. Usually this guidance is personal and meant for the devotee only. Therefore, care must be taken to refrain from insisting that it is revelation for everyone.

In this case I am sharing because I was told I should. Whether the reader wishes to accept it as my thoughts or God's thoughts, it is my belief that this material came directly from the higher source as a demonstration that the journey to inner space is not to void and nothingness but to the Source of wisdom, inspiration, and truth.)

"You must begin now to determine what you really want most of all. So you want a healthy mind, a healthy spirit, a healthy body? Do you want to be gloriously alive, radiantly happy, sustained by wisdom and faith, at peace with yourself and with the world? Then what you want is the kingdom of God, and if you will obey the inner promptings that put you in search of that mysterious realm, you will come into a new lease on life. But you must seek this kingdom first, making it your highest priority. Then with all the vitality, power, and happiness that comes to you as a by-product of the kingdom will come every needed thing. This is one of the most important rules for you to learn, seek first my kingdom."

"So little is asked of you, and yet so much is waiting to be given. If you will faithfully keep an appointment with me, coming regularly for a time of quiet listening and silent adoring, you will have all the help, wisdom, and protection you could ever need. You have accumulated much dreary mental baggage that needs to be put down. Release me within yourself so I may help you on the path of your own inner overcoming. Do not be afraid or angry over any picture in the outer world—turn to me instantly. I walk with you every moment. I will not leave you. I will show you how to keep from dwelling so much in the outer realm that you become unsettled and confused, and I will show you how to bring peace and order into the chaos and conflict of the outer.

"This place within you, the deep center where I AM, is like a lake that is perfectly calm. The surface of its water is not ruffled. Here you will find a profound, eternal peace, the grandeur of a stillness that will put to flight all your fears and frustrations, that will help you reorder your priorities, that will keep your lamp burning brightly.

"Save nothing. What I give you is to be shared. But be cautious in your verbal sharing. It is foolish to cast the pearls of a high, holy experience at the feet of one who is not spiritually prepared to understand it. You can best share the light by *being*. I will tell you when and where to translate that light into speaking or writing.

"So I say to you again, come into the calm and luminous silence and be renewed. Stillness is the very soil in which your higher life grows."

"Today I would ask you to give me charge of your physical being. I want you well, for a strong, whole body is

Water from Deep Wells

the instrument through which your mind and spirit function at their highest level. Some have received the burden of physical suffering and are bearing a part of the world's agony in their bodies, but this is not required of you. Right now it is too much for you to understand why others must suffer. You may ease that suffering, however, even while you do not understand its reasons. What I ask is that you keep yourself strong by constantly charging every cell and atom of your being with my holy light.

"Let this beam of white light now play across your shoulders and neck where tensions and worries often accumulate, causing muscular stiffness and glandular soreness. Feel the light release all your tenseness. Let this light move gently into the inner recesses of your sinus cavities, probing all blockage until you drain free. Let this light examine your eyes, moving behind your eyeballs and purifying these precious instruments of sight that I have given to you so you may look out on this world with pain-free, love-filled eyes, seeing it as I see it. Continue to sit in the silence as this light moves in gentle probing insistence over and within your entire body. Wherever you have a sense of discomfort or ailing, let the light penetrate that spot until the hurt begins to fade. Feel this light sweeping from your toes to the top of your head and back again, penetrating to your very 'withindom' and filling you with the tingling lassitude of perfect health. Know that as you submit yourself to this divine x-ray of love energy, you are being recharged and renewed physically, so that you may walk forth to do my work, free from bodily pain or physical restriction. Your body is the holy temple of the Spirit, and I would have it whole so that it will be out of the way to allow you to function as a channel of my light and love to this world. Bathe yourself often in this light, for this not only keeps you strong, it makes you a freer channel for my Spirit, for through you I would heal others. Go now in the fullness of health, and I will do the work through you that is your divine assignment."

Journey to Inner Space

"Rest here with me for a little while. You are tired and anxious over many things. You are busier than I want you to be. It is not my will for you to be so burdened. I want you freer, brighter, happier. Begin now to consider which activities you should drop and how you might reorder your life so there will be greater periods of relaxation and carefree ease. When you are weary, you are ineffective in the work I want you to do. You must learn when to say no, when to shut the door, when to take care of yourself. There is a definite division between service and surrender, between work and play. Each is needful, yet often in your zeal you allow service to crowd out your time for surrender, and you neglect play in favor of work. There is a balance to be achieved, and I will help you find it. Come to me regularly for instruction. Stay with me long enough to feel your body, mind, and spirit at rest. Turn all your activities over to me. You are not responsible. I am. I will show you what you are to do, how you are to do it, and when you are to do it. I will also give you the necessary strength for every task. But you must remember to allow regular rest periods for your soul, mind, body."

"Today you were unkind to John. You imagined yourself too busy to give him a friendly word, a moment of your time. I know that he drains you, annoys you with incessant chatter, and depresses you with constant complaints. But stop a moment and think what you would do if you were to change places. Would you be any better? There is very little in John's life to give cheer and happiness. He is crying out to you for light. I would have you hold this lost one in my light, for his way is dark and hard. If you will do this faithfully and if you will give just a few moments of cheer each time you meet him, you will help his way become easier and you will free yourself from the added weight of irritation and impatience. Is it too much to ask you to love this one who has grown unlovable? There is no one who needs it more. Give him your mercy, and my mercy will be given to you."

Water from Deep Wells

"Sometimes it will seem to you that these meditative moments bring no new insights, no bursting flashes of revelation. That is as it should be, for such experiences can be both debilitating and unsettling if they come too frequently. Much growth is taking place within you, even though you are not aware of it. Every seed must have its own time of quiet darkness before it can germinate and push forth to the light, so do not be impatient if outwardly nothing seems to be happening. Relax in my love and trust the process that I have ordained. It is not necessary for you to dig up the seeds to see if they are growing. They are, for growth is the law of life. Your responsibility is to tend the garden. Water it from wells of living water, then stand back quietly and gratefully while the light does its own work. In due time the seed will burst forth and bear the fruit of all these months of quietly abiding in the silence. Every moment you consciously surrender to me is filled with growth and good for you and all the world, whether you know it or not."

"These periods you lay aside for me each morning are the most important ones of your entire day. Here you are giving me the opportunity to place the mantle of peace on your shoulders, to gird you with the breastplate of righteousness, to clothe you with garments of holy love from on high, and to fill you with a deep, pervasive peace and contentment. Do not be dismayed over conditions in the outer world. It is too much for you to understand right now. I am aware of the suffering of my children and the plight of my world, and I am doing something about it. Your work is not to agonize over any outer condition; your work is to bless it and bring the light to it. You are ineffective in doing this if you are weighed down with the burden. Do not use this quiet time to mourn over problems in the visible world; use it to rejoice in the truth that greater is the One within you than all that is without. Rest now and let me strengthen and bless you, for I have chosen you for a great work, and I want you well and strong. I need you, and I will not desert you. I love you and I will never let you go. Rest. Abide. Trust. Even though you may not know it, the universe is unfolding as it should."

"You fret and chafe over what seem to be delays in your life and in the outer world. I say to you, there are no delays in the eternal. Everything moves at its own rate and into its own sphere of fulfillment at the right moment and in the right way. You can no more hurry this process of fulfillment than you can move the stars about in the heavens. The rose opens in its own season; the butterfly escapes its cocoon at a foreordained moment. Trust your own seasons and the divinely ordained plan. Only by coming to me and giving yourself into contemplative silence will you be able to see that I am in control, that I will ultimately have my way, and that time is not a factor for me. Learn to live in cooperation with my plan. It is true that you can slow down and deter your own spiritual progress by a refusal to live close to me, but remember that the greatest spiritual lessons the prodigal son learned were those that came to him while he was in the far country apart from the father. This is not to say that you grow best by turning from me. That is utter foolishness. But I am bringing growth to you in every situation and circumstance; there is no place where I am not, no realm beyond the pale of my being. You have one overarching and all-encompassing responsibility—abide in me. Bring yourself daily, even hourly, to moments of consciously abiding in my presence. Soon you will begin to see that there are no delays, it only seems so. Everything is moving in an orderly predetermined fashion toward a great good. The rate of movement may vary for each person, but that is of no concern or consequence to you. It is enough for you to know that I am bringing good out of all things and into all things.

"Recall the long years of delay that came between the time the dream to write was planted in your heart and the time when you first saw your words in print. Once you viewed that time as a frustrating delay, a hindrance to your freedom. But I was doing a special work in you during that time, refining your spirit to a state of radiant acquiescence, until you were able to aver with sincerity, 'It matters not if a single word of mine is ever published, as long as I may know the abiding reality of the eternal word.' You see now that that period was not delay but infinite progress. I planned it that way for you, so rest in my purposes and trust my timing. Then everything will come in exactly the right way and at exactly the right moment."

"I would speak to you of accidents. Everyday you witness what from a human point of view appears to be an accident. When you are wiser and better able to take the eternal view, you will see that just as there are no delays, there are no accidents. Nothing is by chance. Everything is a careful, orderly outworking of the law of sowing and reaping. The Master said what you give out you will get back. You choose your circumstances and select your situations. Some find it impossible to believe this, and it will do no good to tell such persons that they are responsible for what happens to them. It is too much for them to handle in their present consciousness. I am speaking now to you. You are coming of age spiritually, and it is time for you to understand that what is often referred to as an accident is really the product of human failing, human weakness, human perversity.

"But what about the innocent? you say. What of those who suffer unjustly at the hands of the wrongdoer? There is no such thing as pure innocence, even in a tiny babe. Every soul carries within it the scars of centuries of wrong thinking and wrongdoing. There is a karmic law of indebtedness that many are now working out, having voluntarily accepted a path of suffering that will forge a higher evolution of the soul. Everything is for learning; nothing is wasted or useless. I know this is difficult for many to believe. But is it easier to believe that you are in this world without protection, a victim who must suffer mercilessly at the hands of some blind, capricious evil force? No, I tell you there are no accidents. Everything has cause and reason, and ultimately everything has in it the seeds of good. I am bringing forth the good from all things to those who will give me the opportunity to do so.

"I also say to you that you have protection. You are not alone. I have assigned guardian angels and invisible protectors to your pathway, and the Christ is always with you, lifting you to a higher way and helping you overcome and be free of any burden from the past.

"This is not an easy lesson, but it is the eternal truth of your being, and the sooner you accept it the sooner you will be free to use your experiences rather than letting them use you."

"Let me illustrate yesterday's lesson with an example. The cross of Jesus was no accident. Human willfulness and ignorance deliberately erected the cross and nailed him to it. Yet Jesus also chose the cross. His loving way of life produced the inevitable outcome of his death at the hands of those whose lives stood condemned by that love. His enemies had to either change or silence him. They were not able to do either, for real love cannot be silenced. It speaks through the thunder of silence more powerfully and convincingly than all other voices of sounds. The life of Jesus is stronger today than ever. And this is no mere accident."

"Today I would thank you for a service of love. You went forth in the storm to dig away the crusted ice and clean the accumulation of waste from the bird feeder, and as you left the feed, a dozen or more of my little feathered creatures flew forth and ate gratefully of that which I provided through you. They had been waiting for you. Did not you see the shivering brown towhee who hopped to your window and called for you to come out? I love these little ones, and it grieves me that many of my human children are careless or cruel to the creatures of the nonhuman world. I have stirred a great love in your heart for my creation, and I would have you take seriously my commission to treat all life gently and considerately. All the creatures that I have created respond to love and will return love if it is given to them in sincerity. Therefore, do not count it a weakness that you love the animal world. It is a great strength and source of joy.

"Nature spirits are with you often, and it is their love for you and dedication to your mission which evokes a tenderness essence in you for all nature, animals, and all facets of creation. Blessed are those who treat creation with meekness, for they shall inherit the goodness and love of the earth."

"Within the center of infinite quiet lies resolution to your greatest wisdom and action. If you will come regularly and often to this place of peace, you will be saved from much futile and irresponsible behavior, for here I will teach you, correct you, and offer you direction. But I will never force anything on you. What is given is only that which you permit yourself to receive.

"You wonder why few seem to grasp the meaning of true religion, while seemingly the hearts of all are hungry for it. For centuries people have sought comfort and protection through formalized religion, dogmas, and liturgies, and they have left the real work of religion to the teachers. This is fundamentally wrong. If one seeks freedom through faith and peace through religion, he or she must assume responsibility for his or her own development. It cannot be left to teachers. The only teacher to be wholly sought is my Spirit, and that Spirit is within you at the place of your own inner seeking.

"Your assignment is not to follow any earthly teacher or guru on the earth path. Your assignment is to discover the Christ within you. I have given you earthly teachers to assist you in arriving at this place of higher consciousness, but do not rely solely on their truth. Use their teachings as a springboard to your own truth and learn to live by what is verified in your inner being. Teach yourself. Be your own master. Be your own healer. Find the Christ within.

"Do not be impatient with my children who do not understand this teaching and do not turn aside from those who come to you for instruction. But always make it clear that you are not their teacher, you are only the fellow-seeker on the pathway with them. They have access to the same truth and the same light that you have. Do not imagine either that you are out in front of anyone, for this is a form of spiritual pride that attempts to rate spiritual development on a comparative scale. It is not necessary to do this, for the only valid comparison of your growth today is by where you were yesterday. Let others be where they have to be. Love them, bless them, and share with them when it is right to do so, but never allow anyone to deify you or make an idol out of you. Ministers and evangelists often fall into this trap, and it is at that point they cease to grow. Everyone is a seeker, a learner. Those who are called to teach must always remember they are but the vessel for my word and that even while teaching they are the student, learning to listen to me and offering themselves as the channel through which I do my work.

"As you learn to lay aside your judgments of others, learn also to cease judging religions, denominations, or any theological system. I have a higher purpose for you. There is good in every religion, yet each lacks complete truth. Yes, even in Christianity, as it has evolved, there is error and deviation from the pure truth that Christ spoke. You must learn to lay aside all the trappings and accouterments of organized institutions and man-made religious systems and rise above these into a universal religion. No longer think of yourself as Baptist, nor even as Christian. You are more than these. Jesus rose above all such limitations and became the only begotten Son. He transcended all religions. Follow him to the Christ of your own being. As you do, you will rejoice in the new freedom that arrives when titles and distinctions are dissolved."

"I sense in you today a loneliness, a fearful longing, a pervasive discontent that seems causeless to you. Partly this is because you have separated yourself from me by neglecting this quiet time, and I have had no opportunity to give you the reassurance and inner peace that you need. These are difficult days for you. You have allowed yourself to be too busy. Many are making demands on you, for they sense your vulnerability. There are also dark forces in your path right now, and these are stirring your heart with unease. These forces need not be feared, for in my light they will dissipate. Indeed, even now they disappear. Stay in the light until you feel the old familiar peace invade and until your inner strength has returned. I do not tempt you. I lead you from temptation. But I can only do what you will permit me to do. When you come to me for a quiet time you are giving me your permission to help you. Would a hungry child refuse food or a tired body turn away from a bed? Come to me as simply as you go to your table at mealtime or to your couch at nighttime, and I will nourish and renew you from within. Now that you have sampled the joy of living close to me, you will never be able to be separated from me without experiencing intense loneliness and anguish. Do not question my love for you. I love you beyond all power of comprehension, for *I am you*."

"Do not be discouraged if your progress seems slow and if you are not able to overcome everything at once. This is spiritual greed, and it must go. It has taken you a long time to realize intellectually that there is a higher realm of consciousness; the rest of your life must be devoted to attaining it until it is no longer something you think about, but it is what you are. Keep moving steadily and wholeheartedly in the direction of the light. You are loved, infinitely and totally, and you are held, tenderly and carefully, in my embrace. Your awareness of this truth is worth more than any scholasticism or pendantry to which you might aspire; it is worth more than any professional achievement or material success; it is worth more than all *the world's acclaim. Within you at this very instant is everything you could ever need or want. I cannot give it all to you at one time, so I shall give it to you in portions that you can receive and assimilate.* Just remember that there is nothing outside of you that can grant you what your soul desires. It can only come from within. If I repeat this to you often it is because I want you to understand it as the inviolate law of your being. You shall know the truth, and the truth will make you free."

"Though I admonish you always to be the student, the learner, even as you teach, I do not mean for you to ignore the divine authority that is yours. I am in great need of those who will call forth the light into troubled situations and who will speak with my authority the word of peace to a troubled world. This divine authority, which contains the power to sway the universe, only comes to those who are totally yielded to me as a channel of my love. Give yourself to me, and every word you speak will be potent with my power, for it will be my word expressing itself through your flesh."

"Find in the ground of your own being that which can transcend everything external in your environment. I am God of both darkness and light, and if you touch me, you touch the power to transcend even your darkness. In this truth your present disappointments and sense of defeat will pass away. Likewise, all human categories will fade, and a door will open between you and all humanity that cannot be shut. There can be no lines of division drawn. Let your life be a testimony to the oneness of humanity. It matters not what people are called—Baptist, Catholic, Hindu, Jew, black, white, homosexual—they are all my children, and anyone who proclaims division against any or seeks to remove a person's right to be is committing a sin. I want you to preach this oneness, to hold it up before the world as my call to unity and togetherness. In the end this witness to the oneness of all people will undermine any barriers that presently exist. I abhor the lines of separation that have been drawn, for these are the greatest offense to my name and the most grievous of all sins committed by my children. Do not be misled by sincere but misguided Christians who preach against some of my children and place impossible demands on them before allowing them participation in my kingdom. They do so out of fear; but perfect love casts out fear. I have created everyone, and my grace flows through no exclusive channels or conditioned circumstances. It belongs to all my children. This vision of oneness is an innate spark in your being. Fan the spark into a flame. There are few causes worth dying for—this is one. And remember, you are not alone. Those that are with you are more than they that be against you."

"Stop belittling yourself. Humility of self does not mean degrading the self. A true knowing of your frailty and inadequacy is only for the purpose of making room for the immensity of my indwelling. Jesus never once belittled himself. A true son or daughter never does. Step forth in confidence and radiance. You do not walk alone, and you have within you a spiritual giant, greater by far than your present consciousness is ready to admit."

"I sent a particular leadership assignment to you. You spoke to me about it, and I said, 'Go. I want you to do it.' Then you spent much of your time in dread anticipation, partly because you felt inadequate and partly because you did not want to go. Those two elements of your nature, a self-demeaning strain and a rebellious factor, are enemies to your own good. For when you stepped forth to do the assignment and claimed my presence and strength, you were filled with a great peace, a sense of adequacy as you carried it out, and a feeling of satisfaction when it is over. When will you learn to trust me more fully? I will not put you out on a limb and then cut it off. Nor will I send you forth alone and without resources. I need you, and I will supply you with every needed thing. I will give you the words to speak when they are needed, if you will *remember your way* out of your fear and perverseness back to me. I love you. You are a special channel for my word. Trust me more."

"You watched the wind wrench the leaves away from their last reluctant hold on the tree, lift and carry them into the air in a mad vagary of current, and then deposit them in cruel abandon against the stone wall of your garden where they will die and return to the soil. And you asked yourself the question, 'Is this what life is all about? When we finally abandon ourselves to its adventuring call, releasing the womb of security that nourished us to fling ourselves into the dance, are we then only to be crushed against the impenetrable wall that stands between us and our highest aspirations?'

"Although nature is your handbook, teaching you all the spiritual and physical laws of your existence, you have a greater destiny than a leaf. Have I not told you that you are the branch connected to me through Christ the vine? The leaves are produced in the same manner that thoughts are produced, and they live but for a season. When they are released, the way has already been prepared for the new leaf (thought) to come, and the old leaf goes forth to be the nutrient for the soil that will grow the new leaf (thought). Your confusion occurs because you begin to imagine that the leaf is your source instead of the tree. You look to the leaf for fulfillment rather than to the tree. The leaves you put forth will always come in perfect sequence and order as long as you draw your nourishment from the tree. If there appears to be a wall between you and your highest aspiration, it is because you have mistakenly thought the production of the leaf to be your aspiration. Always there will be disappointment and frustration until you understand that abiding in the tree must be your aspiration. Keep close to your Source. Spend much time drawing nourishment and supply from that which is closest to you;

then you will not need to worry about producing leaves or what happens to them. The perfect law of demand and supply will take care of them. The only wall you must concern yourself with is the wall of your own thinking that imagines you to be separate from the Christ, for this is the only wall there is. When all sense of separation has been removed from your thoughts, the walls in the outer world against which your leaves are hurled will disappear like magic.

" 'I am the vine, you are the branches. He who abides in me, and I in him, he it is that bears much fruit, for apart from me you can do nothing. If you abide in me, and my words abide in you, ask whatever you will, and it shall be done for you.' Read the fifteenth chapter of John and ponder the meaning carefully. I have more to say about this."

"Let us continue our lesson about the tree and the leaf. The conflict that has long existed in the world is because my children have imagined they have selves of their own. Each wants to be something of himself or herself, and each enters into conflict with another.

"Think for a moment of the apple trees, bursting now into full bloom. There may be hundreds of apples on your trees because of those blossoms, but there is only one life—the tree. Apart from the tree the apple has no life in and of itself, and the moment the apple is picked, it begins to die. The same rule applies to the branches. If you cut off a branch of the tree, it too begins to die. It cannot exist apart from the tree. There may be many branches, but there is only one tree, one life, one source of supply, and no branch of a tree can ever be in conflict with any other branch of that tree and live.

"Planted at the center of the earth is an invisible tree of life which is the central source of life. You are one of the branches on that tree, and though you appear to be a separate branch, you are bound to all the branches by your connection to the tree. Everything receives its care, its supply, its love, and its protection from the same Source.

Your problems begin when you start to believe that you are separate from the tree. You become anxious, competitive, and fearful. You go out into the world searching for what you need and want, and you enter into a futile struggle of trying to take from others what you think is yours. Yet the simple truth is that what is yours will come to you beautifully, simply, and completely, as long as you remain connected to the tree and do not try to live as a separate branch. No power can hold back what is yours or send to you what is not yours, if you abide in me!

"The Christ is the tree and you are the branches, and I, your God, am the tree-keeper. There is no need to struggle and fight against one another if you remain united in the tree. That is why I constantly urge you to take this inner journey to your Source, to that invisible tree to which you are connected, a tree that is tended by me and from which flows forth all my good. It is not your work to grow the leaf or produce the fruit. Your work is to abide in me and let me bring forth the fruit that waits to be harvested from the richness of your abiding life.

"This is a basic, fundamental lesson that I teach to all seekers and to those who look within themselves for the truth. I teach it now to you. Abide in me. Stay in the place of your connection to me in a state of hopeful expectancy and watch as your fruit grows."

" 'Why am I not getting this thing that I want very much?' This is the question that you have been asking. Let me help you understand it. Yes, I have heard your prayers for this thing, and I want you to have it in its own season. There is first some work to be finished within you, work that is closely allied with this very thing that you want. To grant your request now would be to delay the work. You must surrender your request, so that no matter what happens you can be content with the outcome. Do you want this request granted more than you want my presence? Which do you want more? These are questions you must answer honestly.

"Remember the rich man who came to Jesus asking how to inherit eternal life? He had observed all the commandments, but he lacked one important thing. He lacked the full desire to put me first. He loved his possessions more than he loved me.

"I will grant every request of your heart when your requests are pure and unalloyed, springing from a heart that loves me more than all else. All that I ask from you is an awareness that I am aware of you, that I have an immense love for you, and that I want a greater good for you than you could possibly order or descry. The only way this awareness can come to you is for you to dissolve yourself and your requests into that limitless space within where my peace, my love, and my salvation lie. You see the failures more clearly in your friends and acquaintances than you do in yourself when they do not act on their inner wisdom. I am not asking any great effort of you. I am only asking that you surrender your requests and your greeds to me so that I may refine them. Yes, there is some spiritual greed that needs to be transmuted. I would have that murky darkness within you melted away completely so that your spirit can dwell in pure light.

"The light within you is strong. It is the chimney of the lamp that needs to be cleansed so that the light may shine through. Come to me often and give me the desires of your heart. Turn them over to me with no orders and no demands. I will fulfill them after I have cleansed you from within, so that the granting of the requests will bring you greater good. If with *all* your heart you truly seek me, you shall ever surely find me. And in that finding will come your heart's desires."

"Sometimes you continue to feel that nothing is being accomplished in your times of quiet, that you are regressing rather than progressing. You must lay aside such unsettling thoughts, for you are not able to make an accurate assessment of all that is happening to you. It is sufficient for you to know that no time in the silence is ever wasted. Keep in mind these facts. Creation is not a static condition. New creation is always springing forth within you as you provide the place for God to manifest within your consciousness. Silence is that place, that environment where I work. You are not working alone. Other great lives are also helping you develop that environment of silence where the God-consciousness can dwell. What you are actually doing when you take the time to sit in the silence with every fiber of your being directed toward me is to expose your soul to a higher cosmic energy. This exposure is like the rays from a sun lamp. It will not be felt immediately, but change is definitely taking place. It is leading you out from limited consciousness to an awareness that boundless energy lies dormant within you.

"As you learn to externalize this energy into your outer environment, you will see reflected back to you the growth and progress that has taken place on the interior. Ultimately there is no separation between the inner and the outer, for all energies inherent in an individual are also inherent in the universe. Through prayer and meditation the individual divinity of your being unites with omniscience, and the microcosm becomes one with the macrocosm. As this is accomplished, and although the process continues to repeat itself, it takes place on higher levels as you learn to abide in the stillness. So do not presume nothing is happening in your quiet times, just because you cannot see it. More is happening than you can possibly know, and all of it is for good."

"I give now this message through you to all my children.
"Distorted preceptions of who you are causing your sense of lack and also your inappropriate behavior. If you could perceive yourself as a holy son or daughter and likewise perceive others as holy, you would have no needs of any kind and your behavior would always be under my authority. As a holy son or daughter you have everything. Your awareness of that truth will restore everything to you that you have momentarily lost. Recognize your full

dependence on me, and you will know the full power of a son or daughter living in a true relationship with me.

"You are on this earth working through the illusions of time and space in order to express more fully your spiritual potential. You can delay this process, reduce it to temporary nothingness, or live in partial paralysis if you choose to do so. But you cannot destroy your spiritual potential, for you did not create it. I created it, and what I created cannot be destroyed. Ultimately that spiritual potential must be expressed and released for ultimately you must come back home to me. When you return is up to you, but the delays only create greater confusion, fear, and unhappiness. You are all in a state of returning home. This returning can be hastened if all individual sense of separation from me is corrected. Any lack that exists is of human making and springs from the distorted perception of yourself. You have everything you need, for indeed there is no such thing as lack in my house. Correct your thinking about yourself, confess that you are my holy son or daughter, and as you change your perception of yourself you will find yourself in a state of grace forever, a place of receiving your rightful inheritance. This is one of the most important lessons I will give at this sacred place of your inner knowing. Return to it often until you have learned it thoroughly, for it is the stepping-stone to the stars."

Benedictus,
a Final Good Word

Robert Louis Stevenson once said, "To travel hopefully is a better thing than to arrive." In the spiritual realm, insofar as our vision now extends, there is no such thing as final arrival. There is always another step to take, another lesson to learn, another peak to scale. Since we cannot see our arrival, our best choice is to travel hopefully. This is the benedictus, the blessing, of the journey to the vast invisibility of our inner space—it never ends, there is always something more. In that hope we dare to pray:

> Lord God, I go forth accepting the life you have given me as a joyous, beautiful thing, sometimes mysterious, sometimes transparent, but always challenging. There have been times when I understood it, times when I did not. There have been times when I realized its essential meaning and times when I messed things up. But I refuse to allow those times of mistakes and misunderstandings to get in the way of my taking hold of this great adventure of life that you have given me and living it as fully and completely as I can. So today I accept life with all its fragility, all its wintry darkness, all its forked roads, and all its awesome grandeur and amazing grace. I go forth on the path I chose when I decided to follow your Son Jesus Christ, asking only to be resolute in my determination to see things more clearly, brave in the face of my trials,

uncomplaining at the time of my crucifixion, and worthy to share in the resurrection of new life which has been promised to all who put their hand in yours while walking this earth path.

I travel hopefully, because I believe that you are loving me and waiting for me to come home, that even now you are planning a homecoming celebration when I arrive that will leave no doubt that I am fully accepted, no more a stranger or a transient, but your child in the kingdom of being. I travel hopefully, because I believe that the real of me will not die on this life journey, and when I am finished here, I will go on to new worlds, singing the songs of the unexplored countries. I travel hopefully, because just as I believe I will never die, I believe I was never born, I believe myself to be forever and eternally part of you and that birth and death are just the steps whereby I enter and leave this mortal sojourn. But if I am wrong, I am not sorry for the hope I have carried nor the faith I have nurtured, for I have had the companionship of immortality and the joy of infinite presence, even through the valley of the shadow of mortal death. I travel hopefully, because I dare to believe that someday you, O God, will find me with you and in you, just as I have found you with me and in me. This is the all and the only of my life that sends me forth in quest of you—not to a mountain or to a temple or to a far-off country, but within the inner space of my own being, so that wherever I am, there you will be also. Amen.

On the morning that I penned the final words of this book, I heard from my study a steady hammering sound in the trees below my study. Walking out onto the deck, I peered down into the ravine to see its cause. A little boy with a steel pipe was furiously expressing some pent-up force of childish frustration against one of the young trees, striking it ceaselessly and violently.

"Oh, don't hurt the trees!" I implored.

The pounding stopped, and the boy looked all around to see who had spoken. Failing to see me, he called out, "Who are you?"

"It doesn't matter. Just don't hurt the trees."

"Are you a ghost?"

"No, I'm not a ghost."

"Are you God?" A note of wary reverence had crept into the voice. Little eyes still searched furtively. The opportunity was too priceless to ignore.

"Yes!" I answered, and quietly withdrew from sight. There was no more pounding.

Is it too much for us to believe that God is always seeking to appear in this world through us and *as us?* Perhaps if we live close enough to him our lives may become transparent enough and Christ-like enough that they will show a bit of him to this world. It is a possibility for anyone who is willing to take the journey to the inner space of his godhood, to the source of his divinity.

God bless you who have traveled this little way with me. We leave off here, not to stop, but to continue our way from nothingness into existence, from captivity into freedom, from blindness into seeing, from illusion into reality. Though we make mistakes and encounter conflict, we go on. Once the journey begins we are drawn toward its inward intensity with a compelling force from which there is no return. Our travels are fueled by prayers forged at the inner altar of our secret place and given forth to the One who initiated the journey and guides us to its final step and its joyous completion. The journey to our inner space now merges into the journey to infinite space. The real adventure now begins.